"Reads like a thriller… You probably couldn't tell a lot of the stories she tells as straightforward pieces of journalism… And, arguably, you learn far more about this world the way Fazzini tells it than you would in a sober news story."

The Times

"Kate Fazzini is the rare top-level reporter who can make you see, smell and feel a hidden world, not just understand it. Cybercrime (and security) has found its Michael Lewis."

Bret Witter, co-author of the
New York Times bestseller *The Monuments Men*

"Written almost like a novel, *Kingdom of Lies* offers a vivid account of how these gangs of black hat hackers spreading from Romania to China extort money from individuals like me and the most powerful Wall Street banks, and how the white hats are trying to stop these people who can halt global companies in their tracks and produce digital campaigns to sway popular opinion."

The Times

"Kate Fazzini has crafted a gripping page-turner that is all too timely and real. Good luck putting it down—or going to sleep once you do."

Marc Guggenheim, producer of *Law & Order*
and executive producer of *Wizards*

"Kate Fazzini's work breaking complex cybersecurity news down for a consumer audience is critical. She is tackling this unconventional topic by providing an alternative perspective on the threat, actors and convoluted dynamics."

Dr Frederic Lemieux, Faculty Director
of the Applied Intelligence and Cybersecurity
Programs, Georgetown University

"Cybersecurity isn't just ones and zeros, it's also about the people who sit behind the keyboards—something Fazzini describes in vivid detail."

Naveed Jamali, former US Naval Reserve intelligence officer
and author of *How to Catch a Russian Spy*

About the Author

Kate Fazzini is professor of cybersecurity at the University of Maryland, and also teaches in the Cyber Intelligence program at Georgetown University. She is the principal cybersecurity expert at CNBC, having previously been cybersecurity correspondent for the *Wall Street Journal*. She lives in Astoria, New York.

KINGDOM OF LIES

UNNERVING ADVENTURES IN THE WORLD OF CYBERCRIME

KATE FAZZINI

ONEWORLD

A Oneworld Book

First published in Great Britain, the Republic of Ireland and Australia
by Oneworld Publications, 2019

This paperback edition published 2020

ISBN 978-1-78607-826-1
eISBN 978-1-78607-638-0

Printed and bound in Great Britain by Clays Ltd, Elcograf S.p.A.

Oneworld Publications
10 Bloomsbury Street
London WC1B 3SR
England

Stay up to date with the latest books,
special offers, and exclusive content from
Oneworld with our newsletter

Sign up on our website
oneworld-publications.com

MIX
Paper from
responsible sources
FSC® C018072

For Noah and Zahra

This work of mine, the kind of work which takes no arms to do,
Is least noble of all. It's peopled by Wizards, the Forlorn,
The Awkward, the Blinkers, the Spoon-Fingered, Agnostic Lispers,
Stutterers of Prayer, the Flatulent, the Closet Weepers,
The Charlatans. I am one of those. In January, the month the owls
Nest in, I am a witness & a small thing altogether. The Kingdom
Of Ingratitude. Kingdom of Lies. Kingdom of How Dare I.

—Lucie Brock-Broido

Contents

Contents

KINGDOM OF LIES

Before

The Swallows

René Kreutz is only 15 years old, but she's out drinking and dancing in a club on a Thursday after school, in the outskirts of a mid-sized town in Romania.

It's late 2013. They're playing her jam. Carly Jepsen's "Call Me Maybe."

It's the kind of club where the bouncers don't let in too many guys over 18. So she feels safe. And anyway, she's surrounded by her girl-friends. Giggling. Drinking weak drinks.

They dance in a big circle. Occasionally, one will enter the circle and do a particularly silly series of moves, usually something inspired more by their ballet instructor than pop culture. The song is the kind that forces you to bob and weave and shake your hair around, and she does. It's so loud, it's hard for conversation, or really anything else for that matter.

Hey, I just met you.

René shout-sings along with the song. She bobs her head left to right with an ear-to-ear smile. Her auburn hair flies around, smacks her friend in the face. They laugh.

At the same time, far away in China, a government-backed hacker named Bolin Chou, who has been stealing intellectual property from U.S. companies for the bulk of his career, has left his job. He is drinking a cheap beer in a Shanghai bar for expats, having scored a new gig at a big hotel as a dishwasher. The bartender is glaring at him and he knows he'll be chased out soon, since he doesn't fit in with the more upscale, European clientele. He's surprised they served him in the first place.

With his cell phone, he uses the short time he has left to monitor the computers of all the businessmen connecting to the bar's unsecured Wi-Fi network.

He contemplates the possibilities.

And this is crazy.

In Romania, René, who has never met someone from China, bobs left to right and spins.

At the same time, far away in Washington, D.C., Admiral Michael Rogers, the head of the National Security Agency (NSA) and the Central Intelligence Agency, addresses Congress about cyberthreats, contrasting them with nuclear weapons. "That's very different from the cyber dynamic," he says. "Where we're not only going to be dealing with nation-states, but we're going to be dealing with groups, with individuals, when we're dealing with a capability that is relatively inexpensive and so easy to acquire, very unlike the nuclear kind of model. That makes this really problematic."

René has never met an American. She doesn't know about the NSA, nor what an admiral is.

But here's my number.

In Romania, René enters the circle of girlfriends and starts a silly dance. She pretends her drink glass is a microphone and sings along even louder.

Also at the same time, not so far away, in Germany, Sigmar "Sig" Himelman, an influential 30-something cybercriminal, acknowledges that he's burned too many bridges, including with the local police, and is going to need to make a move. He has already disposed of several computers and hard drives. He's not answering his phones, and soon those will be destroyed, too. He's packing his bag and going somewhere else, somewhere safer for hackers who like to innovate: Romania.

René has never met someone from Germany. She's been a bit sheltered. The junior-league clubbing is about as bad-assed as it gets for her. For now.

But in not too long, she'll be a more influential cybercriminal than Sig, a competitor of Bo's, and one of Rogers' new big problems.

So call me maybe.

Also at the same time, Carl Ramirez stands in a room inside a NOW Bank building in Midtown Manhattan that for reasons he has never been able to ascertain is shaped like a plus sign.

He faces a receptionist's desk, long abandoned, covered in a layer of dust. Behind the desk, a wall of glass showcases a vivid seven-story drop to a lower atrium where bankers sit, drinking coffee and eating power breakfasts. Unbeknownst to the bankers down below and many of the bank executives above, the financial sector is about to be attacked by terrorists.

Carl, an unimposing, flat-footed bank executive with an engineering degree from Carnegie Mellon and a Gomer Pyle laugh, has come to the rescue. He is here to save the world.

There is nobody here to greet him. Behind him and to the right and left are three locked doors. His cell phone doesn't work. Even though this floor is filled with employees, the lobby is dead silent.

Carl thinks the scene is like something out of an apocalypse movie, right before the zombies appear. Carl tries the doors again. No luck. Still locked.

He picks up the phone on the receptionist's desk. The handset has been disconnected. In fact, it's been stripped of wires. Four paper clips sit lined up in a row next to two empty three-ring binders, each with a gold-leaf Fleur Stansbury insignia.

It's 2012 and the world is not ending, but four years earlier, someone emptied this desk out in a hurry when Fleur Stansbury dissolved overnight. Fleur Stansbury moved out and NOW Bank moved in. NOW Bank, Carl knows, is one of the biggest banks in the world, by trade volume, by number of branches, by number of customers, and by number of global offices. Pretty much by any standard that you can measure, NOW Bank is absolutely massive. Trillions of dollars flow through the bank's extensive computer systems every single day.

Nobody has bothered to clean up the desk or hire a new receptionist because this floor is for technologists, not bankers. No big-shot investors were going to be received in this office. No swinging dicks of Wall Street here. Not anymore.

Carl grabs one of the binders. Tucks it under his arm. He needs someplace to store his security reports from today's event. A dusty relic of Wall Street seems appropriate. Above him, a fluorescent light flickers. There are dead flies inside it.

Carl holds a binder with a PowerPoint briefing about the matter at hand: A terrorist attack called Operation Ababil is about to be executed. It is a well-planned cyberattack, and will likely be well-executed by a shockingly well-resourced group calling itself the Izz ad-Din al-Qassam Cyber Fighters.

A little history: NOW Bank's cybersecurity team encountered this collective for the first time four months ago, when the group attacked the bank. The group claimed their attack was a response to U.S. policies in Syria and other problems specific to Shiite Muslims. That's when the Izz ad-Din collective took down NOW Bank's main website.

When this happened, the entire corporate side of the bank, including its executives, its board of directors, and its customers, all looked to the NOW Bank cybersecurity team to find out what the fuck had happened. And what the executives found staring back at them were a bunch of nerds with zero charisma and even less *presence* wearing bad, off-the-rack suits without ties. Some of them even wore athletic shoes, not just on their way to work but all day long. They spoke in inside jokes and used weird technical references and spooky-sounding security terms. They were not reassuring.

So for four months, Carl's cybersecurity team went through a sort of front-office boot camp. They learned what a tailor does. They crammed on how to use PowerPoint. They practiced spinning the Izz ad-Din incident to get a bigger budget, which they needed, because all of them were making a lot less than their friends at tech companies and not much more than their friends in government. With that kind of compensation, Carl's boss, Joe, understood, it was getting harder and harder to hire good people.

So here they are, still trying to explain an extraordinarily complex set of circumstances and protocols to a cadre of executives who enjoy a white-glove technology experience in their day-to-day existence. These are people who rarely bother with technicalities, and when they do, they view them as an inconvenience.

Hackers are a notoriously crude lot, and Carl should know because he's one of the best. He enjoys the elegance of the operation's timeline because it gives him a schedule during which to size up his worthy opponent. Not only does whoever put this together know what they're doing. They have *style*.

This is where the battle between NOW Bank and the Izz ad-Din will be fought.

Game on.

Preface

Kingdom of Lies

It didn't take me long in my career as a cybersecurity executive to figure out everyone was lying to me.

The biggest lie of all came at the very beginning: that cybersecurity is hard. Too hard. Certainly too difficult for someone who lacks years and years of deep technical training. That it is no place for writers.

That thicket of incomprehensible jargon alone seemed meant to discourage outsiders like me from entering the field. They told me I could never hope to understand the terminology unless I'd worked around it for a very long time. Unless I had a special and complicated certification. Unless I knew how to take apart and reassemble a computer. Unless I knew how to code in Python and could read it, interpret it, and spot problems on sight.

And if I somehow managed to learn the lingo, the learning curve for the rest of it would prove insurmountable.

Lies, lies, lies.

It's unfortunate, because there is a huge gap between the demand for cybersecurity workers and the people available to fill those jobs. I think one of the reasons for that is because people can't imagine themselves doing this kind of work.

Can you use a smartphone? Make a PowerPoint? Think on your feet? Ever organize a night out to the movies with your friends that went well and nobody crashed their car to or from the event? Welcome to the twenty-first century's hottest career path. Are you able to charm the pants off women? Did you escape an abusive marriage? Have you ever hosted a toddler's birthday party at your home? Honey, I want you on my cybersecurity team.

After reading the stories in this book, you will understand that what makes cybersecurity complicated is the complexity of human beings. So if you know how to deal with people, you can handle internet security. If you understand what makes people tick, not only will you be able to recognize a threat, you'll be one step ahead of your adversary.

During my career as a cybersecurity executive at multinational corporations, a journalist for *The Wall Street Journal* and later CNBC, and a professor at Georgetown University, I've met a lot of fascinating people. From the hackers who perpetrate malicious attacks to the security professionals who try to prevent these incidents from happening, and the alphabet soup of government agencies that do damage control, at the end of the day they're all fathers, sons, mothers, sisters, and spouses. In other words, people just like us. Yes, white hats cross paths with black hats and change alliances more frequently than you might expect, but they're driven by the same desires as the rest of us—even if sometimes it feels as if everyone in cybersecurity is allergic to the truth.

As a professional, I was told a great many lies about the field I have grown to love so much. After becoming a journalist on the cybersecurity beat, I was told even more. Here are a few:

"Let me introduce you to the hacker community."

This lie is usually delivered with a wink and a nod from someone who thinks they know every hacker on the planet. The truth of the matter is, there is no hacker "community."

Sure, the guys who make a splash at the big annual conferences might say otherwise. But every country, every state, every faction, every identifying group has its own community of people who hack computers. Some of them are extremely conservative, others are massively liberal, most fall somewhere in between. Some wear suits and ties and work as lawyers during the day, while others look like everyday citizens and have great people skills as they pursue their idiosyncratic agendas.

Some are good guys who get fed up with the low pay and boring duties and become criminals. Some are criminals who end up becoming good guys. Many start and end their careers on either end of that spectrum.

Some, including many you'll meet in this book, are extremely proficient hackers who have no time or inclination to identify with any community at all.

As a journalist, I was astonished at the number of people who came out of the woodwork to offer me exclusive access to the hacker community. I couldn't help but notice that the members of the source's "hacker community" were often people just like him or her. My point is there are many different types of people working in this field, and I can guarantee you that a lot of them are exactly like you.

Here's another lie: *"He's a luminary in the cybersecurity field."*

He's probably not. Fame and luminescence don't typically intersect in this field. The people I've met who are actual geniuses aren't famous, and most of them don't have social media profiles. They tend not to pontificate on areas outside their expertise.

The people who are constantly headlining conferences and who are so often offered up to me for interviews have less insight than those who stay underground. Anything a high-profile hacker is willing to share typically carries with it a massive and crystal-clear agenda that I've learned to spot from a mile away. Even if a conversation is off the record, the intel coming from top government officials or other marquee corporate cybersecurity names carries little novel information.

The only people who have illuminated the way for me in this world—and in this book—have been genuine practitioners who never held a C-level title. You've never heard of them and because I've changed their names to protect their privacy, you probably never will.

They are luminaries not because of the degrees they've collected or the events they've headlined but because they carry a lantern that guides the path for others. These types of people typically don't have a public relations team.

One of my favorite lies: *"He doesn't know what he's talking about."*

This one is usually delivered by someone who asserts that he or she knows the cybersecurity field better than anyone else. These people will brag that they know what it's like to be a hacker and can do things that no one else in the room can.

I'm always wary of those who try to establish their bona fides by discrediting the expertise of other cybersecurity professionals. The depth and breadth of this field is so vast that everyone who works in it is an expert at some part of it, and I have yet to meet someone who is an expert at all of it. Not even close.

Every view of an incident is informed by the viewer—what he sees, what her level of expertise is—and that changes over time. It's like asking a tourist to describe Times Square, then asking someone who lives and works in New York to do the same thing. Different pictures emerge of the same subject depending on your point of reference.

Then there is the final lie, the one that is the hardest to dispute, the lie of the *Machiavellian technological wonder*. The Lisbeth Salanders and Mr. Robots. The media loves to portray hackers, security experts, and intelligence professionals through a two-dimensional lens: they're either crusaders for good or practitioners of evil, and they all wear black.

I've read countless news articles about people I know that portray cybersecurity professionals as shadowy puppet masters pulling strings with their computer science acumen. For better or worse, I've seen these people go through all the same human experiences as you and I, and I want to tell you about them.

I've been working in and observing the cybersecurity world for the past decade. Some of my contacts are criminals. Some of them skate the line between truth and fiction. To the best of my ability, I've tried to verify that their stories are accurate or, at the very least, plausible.

The profession, as I write this, is made up of about 9 percent women. I know a lot of them, maybe because we are such a rare lot. In order to staff the shortfall of cybersecurity jobs—millions that will need to be filled by 2020—we are going to have to do a better job of recruiting women to the field. This makes it sound like we are up against some sort of serious challenge, but it shouldn't be this way. It's a natural career for women.

Hypervigilance. Risk aversion. The ability to imagine frightening scenarios that nobody else can see based on a series of devastating, cascading factors. Three pathologies so often held against women in business. Three characteristics of so many new mothers. These are enormous assets in the field. Perhaps it's better, I learned, for women who suffer from them to put them to work, to use anxieties to make money hand over fist.

I didn't know when I entered the field that I was going to write a book, I just knew I wanted to know more about these interesting people who were passing in and out of my life. Writing a book has been very different from being a journalist, in that I'm not objective about some of the individuals I write about here. I consider many of them personal friends; some I consider enemies. I have saved their stories for this book.

Ultimately, this book is about control. If there is one common theme in everything that happens to us when we interact with technology, it's our desire to control our environment in a way that benefits us. This desire to come out on top drives nearly every technical decision we make.

Every catalyst to innovate, every curve in the trajectory forward is borne by someone who wants to control something or someone, or everything and everyone. Maybe with technology, maybe with authority, maybe with brilliance or whatever skill they bring to the table. To be the one who holds the reins high on this monstrous beast we've created—that's the prize. At any given time, hundreds of thousands of people are scrambling and punching and grappling for their ins.

Of course, you already know the answer to the question of who is *really* in control. Because you know more about cybersecurity than you think you do.

1.

The Futurethreat

Carl knows that if bank systems are flooded with packets, they won't be able to handle the traffic, web applications will overload, and the bank's websites will go down. People won't be able to bank or pay bills. Twitter will blow up. Call center phones will start ringing like a sadistic chorus. Bank executives will *look bad*.

That's what happened in September. And that's what the terrorists are trying to do now, for a second time.

But it had better not fucking work, Carl has been told over and over these past few weeks. *This can't happen again.*

Carl doesn't care why this is happening, but bankers always want to know why. So, in Joe's report, he explains the reason that the terrorists have provided for their attack, a rationale that makes little sense but was apparently proposed by the Izz ad-Din themselves online: There's an American preacher named Terry Jones who is threatening to burn Qurans and a YouTube video criticizing Islam, and the Izz ad-Din want both to stop. And also Israel. The group has lots to say about Israel.

The Izz ad-Din claim they have waited four months because they are merciful. They delayed their second action due to the U.S. presidential election and Hurricane Sandy.

But that is all B.S.

Because this kind of thing happens to banks all the time. DDoS (distributed denial-of-service) attacks come from aggrieved teenagers and foreign ne'er-do-wells and every class of hacker in between. They are a dime a dozen. Especially after the financial crisis, when a surge of hostility from Anonymous and activists against "the 1 percent" spiked.

Carl and Joe and the cybersecurity team have stopped DDoS attacks many, many times before. The Izz ad-Din are different. They have the skills and they have the hardware. And people. Lots and lots of people. They are not a loosely defined network of 20-something terrorists scattered across Eastern Europe. Not some kids in a basement somewhere. They are an entire nation-state.

Iran, to be specific.

Over the course of the next several days, Carl and a team of five other security professionals battle the bad guys.

Carl spends all his time in the room. They turn the heat down in the room until it is freezing so everyone can stay awake. Somebody keeps bringing up sandwiches from the cafeteria. Executives drift in and out of the room. Some stand next to him, look over his shoulder, and make significant gestures and solemn sighs before leaving again.

They code name the attack Deep Blue, have daily and nightly and sometimes hourly phone calls about it. More and more people get involved. Some of them Carl has never seen before. Some of them, he knows, are consultants not even affiliated with the bank. The longer the attacks go on, the more people get involved in the crisis. And it *is* a crisis. No one has ever seen anything like this before. From the outside looking in, from the inside looking out, one fact becomes obvious to all: The bank's management needs to make cybersecurity a priority. Not tomorrow, not next week, but right now.

As the suits pile in, act interested, and watch Carl sit at the computer and fight the Iranian Army every fucking day, he becomes more detached and more alone. The attacks surpass the skills of his colleagues, relegating them to supporting roles on the sidelines. Carl is a *real* hacker, an extremely good one, and he's seen it all, but never an attack this big.

Then just as suddenly as it began, it ends. Somebody has finally taken down the stupid anti-Islam YouTube video. The Izz declare the war is over. Carl can't believe it. He sits at his desk, fingers poised over the keyboard, exhausted, overcaffeinated, buzzing just a little bit, wondering if it's really over.

Everyone goes home. Carl stays behind, putting together one more security report for the bank's board of directors. They have asked him to predict when the next strike will come. He considers the request and begins to type. "Futurethreat, a type of cyberthreat from a heavily weaponized nation-state . . ."

Carl reconsiders, hits delete. *"Futurethreat" is a garbage term*, he thinks. It was probably invented by some government lunkhead. It will make the bankers' eyes glaze over. He can't have that. He has their attention and he wants to keep it because Deep Blue has created a golden opportunity for Carl and his colleagues' cybersecurity team.

And his boss. Joe Marcella, beloved by his employees, reviled by his superiors, bursts into the room. He has never, Carl has noticed, entered a room any other way. It is what earned him the nickname among some of his colleagues of Kool-Aid Man. Taller and with about 150 pounds on Carl, when Joe opens a door it has the same look and feel of a giant pitcher of punch smashing through a wall.

"Where the fuck have you been? The fucking suits want another fucking PowerPoint about this shit if you can believe it."

Carl smiles. Joe's his friend. Joe is unpolished—to say the least—but he has a way of earning a great deal of loyalty from his employees, which starts and ends with fighting with the higher-ups to pay them very well. Joe won't make it long past the DDoS attacks. He'll be replaced by executives who don't fight hard for good pay, with predictable consequences.

But those days are more than a year away. Right now, Carl is dealing with the fact that the top-level executives at NOW Bank suddenly care about cybersecurity, and the way bankers show that they care is with money.

Carl writes, "Other hostile nations will have used DDoS attacks as cover for entering and persisting on our networks, with the goal of gathering information covertly over long periods of time."

Carl rubs his eyes, closes his laptop. As he walks into the lobby, now dark, he blows on his knuckles like a gunslinger.

At around that same moment, Bob Raykoff, a former Air Force commander, reads some of the text he and a ghostwriter have cobbled together for the next edition of his textbook.

Futurethreats in cyberspace will require that we take some type of offensive action, heretofore under the characterization active defense. The only way to ensure the safety of these active defense measures is to design clear military protocols around them, and to the extent possible, engage other nations—even hostile nations—in creating a more robust international norm for cyberattacks, cyber-reconnaissance and other tactics.

Bob Raykoff was one of the first people to use the term "future-threat." He is working on his latest book and writing a chapter with that name. He is obsessed with futurethreat. He has been watching the DDoS attacks against the banks and wonders who will make use of the distraction caused by the Islamists. The Chinese? The Russians?

Definitely the Russians. Bob *hates* the Russians.

Military men and women who engage the enemy today may give little thought . . . to the damage they may cause digitally. As with military actions from the air or by drone, military personnel may not be significantly or closely engaged with the people who are affected at the other end of their attack. The collateral damage in cyberwarfare, particularly in the private sector, where these battles will most likely be fought, could be catastrophic.

A little over a year from now, Bob will be Carl's boss. Neither of them knows it; nor can they even fathom the possibility. There are a lot of things that Bob knows about cybersecurity, but there are even more things that he doesn't know. But he's right on the money when it comes to the fallout from the DDoS attack at NOW Bank. It will be catastrophic. There will be considerable collateral damage, and he will be right in the middle of it.

From his office in the Washington, D.C., suburbs, Bob considers the futurethreat again.

Definitely Russia, he thinks. *Or China.*

As it turns out, the futurethreat is neither Russia nor China, It is a 15-year-old girl living in the Romanian countryside, dancing to music so loud she can barely hear herself think.

René Kreutz shouts in ecstasy as another wave of her high school friends makes it through the door of a pop-up nightclub in a small Transylvanian town called Arnica Valka. It's a town hardly anyone has ever heard of. It is known mostly as an acceptable place to stop for lunch between Bucharest and Budapest.

René is a little bit drunk. The club is the center of the world, as far as she's concerned. Everywhere else is orbiting around this spot. Around her.

She dances, the eye of a sweaty storm of teenagers, and screams the lyrics to a Bucharest rapper's hit song, spoken in half English, half Romanian, called "Americandrim." It references every pop-culture trope, one after the other: Coca-Cola, MTV, George W. Bush, McDonald's.

I can be what I want to be
Losing my identity

René's friends scream the last line into the sooty air above them. Everything around her smells like cheap liquor and cherry-flavored lip gloss. In fact, René's drink tastes like cherry-flavored lip gloss.

Is there anything more to life than this? she wonders, happily, drunkenly.

There is. A great deal more, in fact. In three years, René, who is no good at computers but who is utterly charming, will become one of the world's most influential hackers practically overnight.

René squeezes next to her friends and flashes a peace sign for a selfie on an old Motorola cell phone.

At around this same moment in Moscow, one of the world's most influential hackers, Valery Romanov, is taking a selfie, too. It's his favorite pose: Valery Romanov, hacker extraordinaire, with stacks and stacks of cash.

Valery is dressed like an extra in an American office-based situation comedy. A short-sleeved, button-down shirt, wrinkled khakis. Blond and pudgy, he isn't really focusing on his own bland countenance. He centers the photograph on the cash instead, the real star of this portrait. He flashes a peace sign.

Romanov has just finished watching the DDoS attack against NOW Bank from inside the bank's networks. He's in there, too. But not for silly Islamist reasons. He enjoys live-action fighting. Like pay-per-view only without the pay. He smiles and contemplates the bottle of vodka beside him.

The DDoS attack presents a big opportunity for somebody, he thinks as he looks at the open ports at the bank, the unguarded sections of a huge, vast enterprise. The data has been left unguarded because the bank is pouring all its resources into fighting the DDoS attack.

Valery notices that all of the credit cards issued by the bank are now expired. Somebody has slipped in while the bank was fighting off the Iranians and made the change. But it wasn't him. Not this time.

Valery is a little preoccupied these days. The FBI is after him. And Interpol. And now the surprisingly fast and frightening Direction Générale de la Sécurité Extérieure in France. He's drinking too much.

His new fiancée is pregnant. The selfies with the cash make him feel better.

Two years earlier, he got caught up in stupid Islamist bullshit when the cafe in Marrakesh he happened to be eating at was blown up in a terrorist attack. Now part of his head is missing. Before that, and for a little while afterward, he was one of the greatest, most prolific, and most influential hackers in the world.

Now it's 2012, and his number is just about up.

2

The Charlatan

Caroline Chan is a killer.

Her new boss doesn't know this. And he won't realize it when he meets her today. In fact, he never will.

Caroline works at NOW Bank, one of the world's biggest banks. She doesn't wear a suit. She's not in Manhattan. She's in a back office in New Jersey and doesn't dress to impress.

Caroline is what is known in the staid language of corporate finance as a business manager, and she manages the business of the bank's cybersecurity. She manages the shit out of it. She does the budget; builds teams of engineers, technicians, security executives; and keeps the factions from fighting with one another.

She also hires the hackers. She's been doing this for nearly 20 years, since she was an intern fresh out of college. She's been hiring hackers since before the bank knew it needed to hire them. She's the hacker whisperer, and they are her dragons.

Caroline is a 4-foot, 11-inch Chinese woman with a New Jersey accent and an Irish Catholic husband. She doesn't crush nuts in board meetings. Her ambition extends to doing good for the people who have become her friends and carving out a comfortable existence in the New Jersey suburbs.

She is always handing the microphone to somebody else. She scoops the ice cream at retirement parties. She drops achievement certificates on her colleagues' desks on their work anniversaries. She's the one who hugs the interns when they are done for the summer. She does all of the dirty work.

But, by God, if you cross her . . .

Caroline incubates and raises hackers. She gets them when they're young, watches them hatch, and turns them into dragons. Many of them grow into productive bank employees, testing the bank's networks, rising through the executive ranks. The bank has 300,000 employees, and they're spread out in all corners of the globe. There's one guy in Greece, three people in Beirut, and a receptionist in Uzbekistan. Her dragons have grown up and spread their wings across the bank's vast expanse. She protects them from the suits. She is the Daenerys Targaryen of cybersecurity.

Take Carl, for instance. He's one of her dragons. Now he's a high-level manager in Singapore. She made sure he was taken care of after the DDoS attacks. She takes care of her dragons when they deliver, and they always deliver.

Nobody has more dirt than Caroline. All those executives who try to score hookers on Craigslist? She knows them on a first-name basis. The traders who create their own applications so they can insider trade? She's onto them. The derivative swappers who lose it from the pressure and send abusive emails to the CIA? She has some stories.

The executive who propositions his employees on one of those "disappearing" chat services? She's got more than a few files saved.

The C-suiter who registered his corporate email with backpage

.com—not to procure a hooker, but to be one? Oh, she's keeping that one to herself for now.

Everyone at NOW Bank who has ever done anything at all related to cybersecurity has worked for Caroline. The senior guys, the junior guys, even some of the big shots who go on CNBC, they all sat in a room across from Caroline once. They slid a copy of their resume across the desk, answered her probing questions, and negotiated their salaries. She dealt with them all with the tenderness of a mother.

After the first round of DDoS attacks from Iran, it was Caroline who polished up the basement dwellers, freaks, and weirdos who saved the day. She made them presentable for the company's board of directors, especially on paper. She made sense of what hackers do with neat charts and tidy graphs, workforce shortfalls and budget projections. Lingo the suits could understand.

She was the one who scored them a brand-spanking-new budget and hundreds of new open positions. It was she who consoled them when the board then made a left turn and hired some new guy to be the top cybersecurity executive, some military guy who spewed a lot of manly stuff about battles and cyberwar that sounded impressive. Someone from outside.

This morning Caroline dusted off her best suit to go to Manhattan and meet the new guy. He has a litany of very impressive titles, but word from her sources is that he appears to know little about the nuts and bolts of the field of cybersecurity, nor, according to them, does he seem to know how a bank operates or what its workers do. Although she herself doesn't trust him, she tells her colleagues to give Bob Raykoff a chance.

But she remains skeptical. She taps into her vast network of corporate hackers for all the intel on him they can muster. He's a glad-hander they say, at best. Stories are already trickling in about how he needs an excessive amount of handholding. For instance, when he travels he insists on having someone accompany him to point out which service car is his. Not once or twice, but every single time. He suggests bringing in an ex-military general at an exorbitant salary to read a weekly report about cybersecurity to bank executives. Presumably *with gravitas*.

Bob Raykoff. A former military big shot. Then a *consultant*. Author of extremely boring academic textbooks, discussing untested theories on the nature of hacking, geopolitics, and cyberespionage.

Give him a chance, Caroline thinks as she smiles, shakes his hand. He seems to be nearly two feet taller than her. His height is not, she knows in her heart, why he looks right past the top of her head as if she isn't even in the room. She gets out her four-color pen and a fresh notebook.

They talk. Well, Raykoff talks. Caroline will be his chief of staff. He doesn't like the title "business manager." Caroline knows the bank calls this function a business manager and not a chief of staff to confer a sort of corporate neutrality to the title. Something more sober and removed than charged and aligned, politically, with the senior-most leader.

Executives are expected to be able to interact with all the people who work in the bank. A business manager is an organizer; a chief of staff is a gatekeeper.

Gatekeepers. They are not just deadly in the enterprise, they are murderous to the practice of cybersecurity. Caroline knows this—everyone in cybersecurity knows this. A 20-year-old analyst who specializes in examining computer code must be able to quickly raise an alarm to his top executive. Gatekeepers stop that from happening. A talented engineer who has unique knowledge about mobile device security must be able to shine when the bank buys new cell phones for everyone. Gatekeepers stop this from happening.

Still, Caroline is a company woman. If her boss wants her to be a chief of staff, she will call herself a chief of staff. But she'll do the job the right way. And she will manage his business. She will manage the shit out of it.

Just before Raykoff came on board, Caroline and the others who had survived the DDoS attack decided to create a matrixed organization. For cybersecurity in the business world, this works well, because there are so few employees and so many things to do. Everyone multitasks.

When a cybersecurity team is matrixed, everyone—including the people who do the hacking, manage the buildings, install the technology, and deal with regulators—cooperates with each other.

What Raykoff proposes is the opposite of that. A heavily layered, top-down organization, where one leader (him) has all the decision-making power and those below him report exclusively to him. This works well in the military, where people must know where their orders are coming from. It does not work as well in a corporation, especially in an organization that does not rely on orders to achieve goals. The enterprise, by contrast, depends on the autonomy of very smart people who are paid to solve problems.

Imagine it this way: You are a cybersecurity employee. You need to make a change to some software that the bankers use. This change will cause the software to go offline for four hours during the workday. The bankers want to be able to work, to make money and hit targets, and they have to do this job using the software. They will be very angry about this. You, the cybersecurity employee, therefore, will not order them to do it because if you do so, they will tell their boss, who will tell his boss, who will raise it up to a high-level manager who will then get into a fight with your high-level manager, delaying this important security project. So instead you negotiate.

You agree with the business unit leaders to stagger the time, so only half the downtime is during the workday and the rest of the hours are on a Sunday. You create a chart describing precisely how the downtime will keep their systems safe from some kind of awful security problem that recently struck traders at another bank. You, the cybersecurity employee, are not in charge. Neither is your boss. Nor are the bankers or their bosses. Nobody is really "in charge" except the shareholders, so all things must be negotiated.

But it becomes quite clear that Raykoff, who continues talking over Caroline's head about operational strategies and synergies and best practices, does not believe this, or perhaps does not understand it. As Raykoff drones on, it becomes clear that Caroline will not be in her job for long, because he wants a military man. Someone more hard-hitting, more authoritative. One of his buddies.

He says he wants to be insulated from the lower levels of staff. He discusses adding several layers below the chief of staff to help with this. He already has a few people in mind. People to replace all the talented people, like Carl, who have already proven their worth.

Gatekeepers for the gatekeepers. Caroline winces.

It's not that Caroline isn't comfortable with leaving her job if necessary. This is the nature of how a bank operates. Organizations change all the time. But she never contemplated having to leave her friends in the hands of someone who so transparently doesn't understand how the organization that hired him works. She feels an unfamiliar anxiety in her stomach as he rambles on. He mentions some aspects of cybersecurity that are unfamiliar to her. She plumbs her memory and experience to try to understand the terms he's using.

It's government jargon. Terms that have little practical application in the enterprise. Then he brags a little, something about having served

as a cybersecurity advisor to Condoleezza Rice. He talks about
something called *con-ops*. Concept of operations. That sounds vaguely
familiar.

"Do you mean a business plan?" she asks.

He stares back at her blankly.

What we have here is a failure to communicate.

It gets worse. He seems annoyed that she spoke. He becomes gruff.
Dismissive. *Rude*. Asks her where the coffee machine is. Makes a joke
about how that's probably sexist. She composes herself. Anger helps.

He asks her whether she knows how to use the fax machine. Her
eyes narrow. Caroline has a master's degree in cybersecurity and seven
technical certifications. She knows more about financial-sector security than anyone at the U.S. Department of Treasury.

He begins listing all the cybersecurity staffers he is hoping to hire,
a job he is tasking her with. The people he is naming will replace some
of her most precious, most loyal dragons. People she loves like her own
family. The godparents of her children. Some attended her wedding.
She cried with them when their children were born and, in some cases,
when their children died.

He never looks at her. He keeps his eyes set on a space on the wall
far above her forehead.

He asks her if she knows the best route to get to the Newark airport.

She is taking notes. She's written the name "Bob Raykoff" in black
as the header. She clicks the black part of her four-color pen closed.
Clicks open the red part. Draws a neat red line through his name.

"Yes, sir," Caroline says with a smile. "I'll go print off a map for you."

On her way out, Caroline stops by the operations center, where
she's greeted cheerfully by some of her colleagues. She gives out a

round of hugs. They want to know how the meeting went. She tells them it was fine. No one says another word. They don't have to.

Raykoff doesn't know it and he never will, but his career at NOW Bank is over. It ended during the first hour of his first meeting with the mother of so many hackers.

It will be a very fast, then a very slow demise.

It is 5:15 a.m. in Vladivostok, Russian Federation, and still the previous day elsewhere—3:15 p.m. in Orlando, Florida, and 12:15 p.m. in Seattle, Washington, and 9:15 p.m. in Tel Aviv, Israel.

Tony Belvedere is at the Orlando International Airport. He waits quietly in a long line of tired, sweaty families. The air conditioner blasts. He contemplates a giant gumball machine the size of a minivan. It has an intricate trail and takes minutes to spit out each individual piece of candy. Two boys keep pumping quarters into it. Tony understands. It's mesmerizing to watch.

He's on his way to Newark. Once he reaches his destination, Tony plans to drive out to a dump of an abandoned suburb of the city, a subsection of a neighborhood called Orange, and set up a fake bank. It's the fifth time he's done this.

He'll set up the fake bank inside the Clarksburg Federal Credit Union, a nearly defunct institution for low-income residents of Orange. For the modest sum of $100,000, he will bribe the credit union's board of directors to allow him and his cohorts to take it over.

He will pay in cash with the proceeds of the members-only sports memorabilia collectors group that he owns. Tony hates sports but loves money. That company, Fantastical Autographs, is a front that launders money for cybercriminals in Vladivostok and Tel Aviv. Using Bitcoin converted into cash, the dirty money gets filtered into phony sports memorabilia investments, then cashed out and cleaned up through a network of both real and phony banks.

Tony's not flying with the $100,000 in cash. That would be gauche. It's in a business account held by Fantastical Autographs at a NOW Bank branch in Midtown Manhattan, just 11 floors below where Caroline Chan sits in a conference room, sadly contemplating what she will do next in her career.

Tony's associates in Tel Aviv, Moscow, and Vladivostok have also hacked into NOW Bank. They prowl the bank's networks, looking around, taking information from the bank's asset management organization about people who may be susceptible to a pump-and-dump scheme. This type of scheme will involve calling those individuals who, based on their data, appear rich and possibly vulnerable enough to hit with a sales pitch for penny stocks. Once their orders drive up the price of the stocks, of which the criminals hold the majority, they will "dump" the worthless investments and pocket a significant profit.

They take just enough information, not too much to trip any alarms, not enough to ping the sensitive radars of the bank's many sophisticated cybersecurity tools. Just enough. Little by little. They drill these folks with penny stocks, then reap the proceeds. Drip, drip, drip.

They've made close to $100 million doing this. Some of that money will be flowing through the credit union by the end of the month; some of it will make its way back through NOW Bank. Some of it will be used to buy baseballs with forged Pete Rose signatures for outrageous prices. None of it will be in any given place at any given time.

It's some kind of god-awful hour in Tel Aviv, but his associates there are awake and texting him secure, disappearing messages on a smartphone application called Wickr. They want to know the status of the bank setup in Orange. They have too much money; they need to dump it now. They don't state this exactly, of course, but Tony gets the gist.

They are not just in NOW Bank. They're in some smaller banks, as well. They've also hacked a consulting firm, an accounting giant. They're even in *The Wall Street Journal*. All with the same goal—finding people with too much money and not enough street smarts. Thankfully for Tony and his cohorts, there are a lot of people who fit that description.

At a place like NOW Bank, it's easy for hackers to narrow the target pool. The bank does the work for them by cordoning off the rich and older customers from the hoi polloi.

NOW Bank has five primary lines of business: retail banking, investment banking, commercial banking, asset management, and the core corporation itself, which is where all the lawyers, human resource people, and technology staff are housed.

The retail bank oversees all of the bank branches, its brick-and-mortar presence. This includes the mortgage lending business, car loans, personal loans, small business banking, private banking, and wealth management. Those last two might be of some interest to the Israelis. The highest tier of individuals served by the retail bank are people who have at least $50 million in assets but less than $100 million. Not *that* rich. But good targets for one-off schemes. The retail bank is a great target if they are going after credit card numbers and checking accounts, but they're not.

Then there's the commercial bank. It's a slightly better target because there are some big transfers going back and forth. This makes for lots of reconnaissance opportunities for other types of operations. Specifically, it's perfect for getting enough information to execute man-in-the-middle attacks.

In these types of schemes, the bad guys get as much information about a company's CEO as possible. They'll pretend to be him—digitally anyway—and convince his lawyer or his secretary to wire money to an offshore account, feigning urgency on an unpaid invoice. Some of these scams make upward of $10 million at a time.

And then there's the investment bank. A treasure trove of embarrassments, especially when plumbing the emails of male traders who just *cannot* keep it in their pants.

These guys have been dreaming of the day that they can have a big swinging dick just as described in *Liar's Poker*. Those days are long gone, but even the 20-year-old upstarts don't realize it. They don't even work on Wall Street. They work on Park Avenue or in Brooklyn. There are 16-year-old Russians turning more profit than they do, and without taxes. These bankers put so much information about what they're doing in email and text messages. Who's acquiring whom, what analysts will say in their next series of letters recommending certain stocks. They store valuable algorithms, business plans, instructions on how to execute high-speed trades, and they do it carelessly. Hubris.

Then there's asset management. Nobody's allowed in without $250 million or more in wealth. This is the sweet spot for a pump-and-dump operation. But it's smaller and more prestigious and, for that reason, harder to get to. That's a lot of money and reputation at stake, and banks have traditionally been better at protecting these clients.

At NOW Bank, as in most large banks, the asset management organization is run by a *personality*: Lydia DeBuffet.

Lydia DeBuffet conveys a very specific type of wealth: confident but never flashy. She's unmistakably beautiful, but not sexy. Grievances are closely held and never, ever aired in public. Lydia is deeply intelligent, aggressively well connected—more than she will ever let on—and she can bevel the edge of a Carrara marble countertop with her glare.

In many ways the asset management network is like her: utterly impenetrable. Unless you have $250 million. Or look like you do. Or, in the case of Belvedere's contacts in Tel Aviv and Russia, have other ways to get in.

Finally, there's the corporate organization. Compared to asset management's refinement, corporate is the Lotto-ticket buying cousin from the old country. Bob Raykoff sits in corporate. When he meets Lydia DeBuffet for the first time, it does not go well. Because one of them holds all the cards—the one who makes the money—and it's not him.

Within the company, corporate is referred to as a "cost center." Meaning it has a negative bottom line and is a drain on resources. Cost centers don't generate revenue, they only incur costs.

Cybersecurity is also a cost center. However, the DDoS attacks demonstrated value in what cybersecurity professionals do. But value and making money are two very different things. People like Caroline will never have the status of a less-experienced banker who happens to bring in the bucks. Most people who work in the corporate setting understand this implicitly, but this reality can take time to get used to.

Technology is both corporate and a cost center. After the financial crisis, the bank had the unenviable task of integrating, practically overnight, the technology from several other large investment banks, retail banks, commercial banks, and asset managers who were thrown together at once—all on a cost center budget. The bank also had to integrate thousands of potentially disgruntled employees who weren't thrilled about the work, a huge risk to cybersecurity.

At about the same time in mid-2014, in a prison cell in Seattle, Valery Romanov contemplates the indictment against him. The indictment is sealed and not yet available to the public, but he knows why he's being held because he has a copy. It's his indictment.

He has been accused of multiple violations of the U.S. Computer Fraud and Abuse Act. He is accused of abusing computers and the internet, two entities he thinks deserve far less abuse than humans. He's not particularly worried. Such crimes normally garner a sentence of five years or less, so it's not like he will be here for decades.

Beginning at a time unknown, but no later than October 2, 2009, and continuing through on or about January 20, 2011, within the Western District of Washington and elsewhere, Valery Romanov, aka NTrain, aka Roman Valerov, aka Nikolai Rubenfeld, aka nCux, aka bandylegs, aka shrork, aka Tokyo Joe, aka peacemaster, aka Tupac (hereinafter Valery Romanov), and others unknown to the grand jury, knowingly and willfully devised and executed, and aided and abetted a scheme and artifice to defraud various financial institutions, including but not limited to NOW Bank, Boeing Employees' Credit Union, Chase Bank, Capital One, Citibank and Key Bank. The object of the scheme and artifice was to "hack" into the computers of retail businesses within the Western District of Washington and elsewhere; to install malicious computer code onto those hacked computers that would effectively steal the credit card numbers of the victim businesses' customers; to market and sell the stolen credit card numbers on criminally inspired websites, for the purpose and with the intent that the stolen credit card numbers would then, in turn, be used for fraudulent transactions across the United States, and in foreign countries. By way of this series of criminal actions, the defendants intended to and did generate and receive millions of dollars in illicit profits that they then converted to their own personal benefit and use.

He scans the indictment again. And again. And again. Reads it in full. Makes a mental note of the things they got wrong, but does not laugh about them. Here, in this cell, they have taken away his computers. There is nothing to laugh about. He has nobody to ping, nobody to text to commiserate with about this injustice. He cannot take selfies with stacks of cash to balm his pain. He's alone with the papers and his own mind.

The printed pages feel foreign to him. He doesn't like how thick and heavy the paper feels, how difficult it is to interact with the words. Sometimes he swipes his fingers across it by mistake instead of turning the page with his hands. There is no depth to it, no endless electronic well to dive into. If Valery Romanov were the anxious type, which he is not, he would be feeling it now. He has reached the end of the 40-page indictment. He goes back again to the first sentence. His favorite sentence:

Beginning at a time unknown.

This is the government's biggest mistake. Because when did it all begin for Valery? What made Valery the most influential hacker in the world? He goes over, in his mind, some of the options, but none of them is a time unknown. He knows all of them.

1984. Maybe that's when it began, when he was born and lived in a 1,000-square-foot room in Vladivostok, Russia. A port town on the Sea of Japan, 5,778 miles from Moscow, a two-day, 120-stop train ride on the Trans-Siberian Railway. He shared the room with his single mother and three other families.

His father left when he was two. He learned how to use computers at a young age. Buried his heart and his life in them. He sank into them more deeply every time his alcoholic mother got drunk and ignored him. She could be sitting in the same room yet be locked far away in her head, farther even than Moscow.

He would grind, grind, grind into the code, plunging deeper into the internet just to see how deep it went. Digital technology slowly but surely began spreading its tendrils everywhere, giving him the pleasure of diving into an ocean that kept getting more interesting as he went. In those early years, it was so exciting to see it grow. Into shops and schools and private clubs, government agencies, other countries, other worlds.

Wherever the internet went, Valery could go, too. Into homes, gyms, and Army installations. Into ATMs and the little tiny boxes where people swipe their credit cards. Especially the little boxes.

He showed unusual proficiency with computers. His teachers optimistically talked about a nice job for him in technology. Maybe he could have a good paycheck right out of high school and help his mother, they said. He had bigger ambitions. To be an entrepreneur. Own a start-up. Have equity.

At the age of 17, Valery came home from school one day and found his mother had drowned in the bathtub. Whether it was deliberate or not made little difference to him.

After the funeral he accepted that his father was never coming back. With nobody left to love or hate, to impress or distress, Valery went in a different direction. Down, down, deeper into the internet, to a place with no bottom.

To his surprise, Valery found himself there. Many selves, actually. Cocky and poetic as his hero Tupac Shakur one day, smooth and cool as Drake the next. He kept stacks of cash in his closet. He drank too much vodka and sang the lyrics to his favorite Tupac song, "Starin' Through My Rear View."

The U.S. government was right. Valery knowingly and willfully invented the machinery that revolutionized how credit card numbers are stolen. Those who noticed a fraudulent charge on their credit card in those early years of the internet may have been reimbursed by the bank, but Valery was in on it, too. Every last-minute Christmas purchase and late-night Taco Bell run, Valery was there. He was inside every swipe of the card. He was everywhere and everyone and nobody at all.

He had a house in Bali, one in Rome, one in Tokyo. That one sat directly across the Sea of Japan from his old single-room dirt pit and the bathtub where his mother drowned in Vladivostok. He had beautiful women. Fistfuls of cash. He had a child with one woman, then another kid with a different woman. Their mothers are ungrateful but good at raising children. An adequate choice. The world is my bitch, *beginning at a time unknown.*

Tupac went to prison, too, Valery thinks. He did around a year, and that was for a sex crime. Computer fraud isn't nearly as bad. Valery hopes it won't be that long for him. He's made some notes for his lawyer. Government agents from four different three-letter organizations want to talk to him.

He knows so much that the government would like to hear, he expects they'll let him out in five minutes with a pat on the back and a nice fish dinner at one of Seattle's finest restaurants. They'll want to learn about the Israelis doing that pump-and-dump scheme. He can describe to them precisely how he laundered his money. Give up some people he can characterize as big shots but who are, in reality, nobodies.

He has taught so many. Across Europe, Asia, the former Soviet states, America, too. He wasn't just a carder, he didn't just scam numbers, he was an *educator.* The people he instructed branched off, started their own operations, modified the code, and found their own niches to exploit. There are people who can modify the card-creating machines at banks, insiders who get jobs as restaurant servers to install malware on their busiest terminals. Swipe, swipe, swipe.

One of his most lucrative operations was in gift cards. He and his contemporaries used stolen credit card numbers to buy reams of the cards, then used those cards to buy commodities that could be cashed out. Tires, iPhones, gold, it didn't matter. They bought and bought and bought. The government will want to know who those people are, he imagines.

Right now, he just wants to go back to Vladivostok and sit in a big room with a laptop warming his thighs and a very good internet connection. He is inside nothing now. He is outside. The analog world is strange and stupid. He hopes he won't be out there for a whole fucking year. *No way he would get a whole year,* he thinks.

Valery is right. He won't get a year. He'll get almost 30.

Back at NOW Bank, Bob Raykoff is perched on an uncomfortable stool in a large conference room in New Jersey. He's meeting his entire cybersecurity team for the first time. Caroline has just handed him the microphone.

His title is chief information security officer. He has two bosses, the chief information officer, who is his boss on paper, and a chief security officer, who was the person who brought him into the bank—another Air Force vet named Edward Smitty. Smitty is fairly new himself. He is there today, standing next to Raykoff. It's the first time many of the bank's cybersecurity staff have met him, as well.

"I have to say," Raykoff says, halfway through his speech, "I wanted to do this job for one reason. I wanted to protect the people of this

country, of the United States of America, and their money, their treasure. That's their treasure, the people of this country, and I take that
job very seriously, and I think it's a very honorable job to protect those
customers."

The speech does not go over well. About a quarter of the people in
the room are from London, where they oversee investments from
European nations. The bank in London has no operations that involve deposits from individuals, and those workers have no American
customers. There are a few people from Singapore who had dialed in
by video conference. One of them looks puzzled and texts his colleague in New York an earnest message:

Is NOW Bank pulling out of Asia??? :-0

This is a problem. As I write this in 2018, at the time of the action in
the book, and before then, too. Global corporations serve masters in
many different countries. Militaries serve masters in one country. Corporations are loyal to their clients and shareholders. Militaries are
loyal to their citizens. Corporations must bow to the rules of the ju-
risdictions where they want to operate. Militaries have strict protocols about showing deference to other nations.

Over the course of the past three decades, the digital battleground
has shifted to take advantage of the muddy boundaries between these
two factions.

Early in the history of hacking, government agencies enjoyed the
relative simplicity of a unilateral back-and-forth—countries tried to
hack them, and they tried to hack those countries back.

But corporations, with their complex international ties and information that proved to be just as valuable as the information being
cached by governments, became much more interesting battlegrounds.

In many ways, the private sector has always been an easier environment to exploit. Surveillance and theft, if done quietly, fly under the radar. Executives don't care if someone takes your money, if they even know, and if they do know, who would they tell and why? What does it get them? They are happy to be kept in the dark.

NOW Bank has major operations in China and Russia. The U.S. government wants banks to share information about nation-state attacks they receive from these countries. But NOW Bank must do business there. How does it reconcile this discrepancy?

When companies realized they were under a direct threat from nation-states, they woke up, but only slightly. They invited in, as NOW Bank did, as many military people as they could get their hands on, thinking that those sources could offer some valuable insights that didn't exist in the private sector.

They were right in one regard. Few bankers have the ability to offer up valuable military battle strategies. Their values are tied up in making money, not in military machinations.

And they were right in another regard: Military veterans make excellent cybersecurity employees, because they understand security so well. They are disciplined. They have insights into perimeter security and intelligence that traditional technologists usually do not.

But bringing in a lot of military brass introduced a great deal of unforeseen conflict, primarily because the criteria for rising to a top military position are not the same as climbing the corporate ranks. There are plenty of ex-military folks working in cybersecurity who have impressive skill sets, but they typically didn't come from the upper echelon.

Then there are the charlatans. Steeped in jargon and tough talk, with little discernible real-world knowledge or experience to back it up, they quickly make a mess of things. In the hierarchal haven of the military, these individuals do just fine. They have countless staffers to prop them up and carry them through, to do research, to write detailed plans, to get coffee and run the printer. But these kinds of people don't flourish in corporations, and most certainly not in cost centers.

Absent all those extra staffers, the charlatans often find themselves revealed in sharp relief. Like a pilot flying with no pants who suddenly has to eject.

3.

The Wall

The customer service rep on the other end of the line can't be more than 20 years old, and she's clearly reading from a script. But Victor Tanninberg's brain doesn't process information in that way.

"I'm never shopping at Home Depot again. These people, their arms grow out of their asses. You know, I just needed a fucking area rug for my fucking living room and now I'm going to have to spend the next fucking week waiting for a new credit card, Jesus fucking Christ."

It's now close to the end of July 2014.

"Sir, as I mentioned, we're sorry for the inconvenience. We can expedite the new card. Unfortunately, there are many ways criminals can fraudulently obtain credit card numbers."

Victor weighs the pros and cons of continuing the argument with the NOW Bank customer service rep.

An hour ago, he tried using his card at his neighborhood Habib Deli outside Princeton, New Jersey, to buy cigarettes and extra-sweet iced tea, and it was declined.

Thirty minutes later, someone from the bank's credit fraud

department calls Victor. Somebody tried to use his card number to buy tires in Germany so the bank locked up the card. Can't unlock it. Have to get a new card. He has another card somewhere in a cabinet or a drawer, for emergencies. Maybe in the freezer? Packed away behind a stack of old, dusty laptops probably. No, stuck between the pages of a theoretical physics textbook on a high shelf. He can't remember.

"Fuck." Victor hangs up the phone.

Victor is a hacker, too. But he's not some scumbag who steals credit card numbers, he's a pro, and these people keep giving him a bad name. Making everyone think all hackers are criminals. He spots a pack of Marlboros, with a single cigarette left inside, hiding in the corner of the pack. Serendipity, at last. *Thank Christ,* he thinks. He lights it up and starts hunting for the spare credit card.

Back at NOW Bank, Caroline is packing a suitcase with clothes and scarves, toilet paper, baby diapers. One of her colleagues, a communications specialist named Frances, had a house fire. She's bringing her the suitcase as a care package. She adds a striped shorts-and-shirt set with a smiling puppy on the front. Toddler size 3.

Something else is going on. It's not the Home Depot thing. That's just a standard breach, like the Target thing before it. This one is different.

A small flame has been started within the bank's security team. A whisper of something wrong. A trip wire tripped. Some of the most technical staffers have been in closed-door meetings. Others, those not privy to the inside story, whisper speculation back and forth. It's something Caroline recognizes as significant. But until somebody who determines who needs to know tells her she needs to know, she will not know. She wonders where Raykoff is on that list, if he is on it at all.

Caroline leaves the suitcase under the woman's desk and walks out of the bank's headquarters, hoping to catch a train back to the New Jersey office before 5 p.m.

After the DDoS attacks in 2012 and 2013, cybersecurity enjoyed an uptick in status at the bank. It gained political currency in the sense that the attacks were so high profile that executives knew promising to do something about them would create professional heft. It also saw an increase in real capital because the attacks were a catalyst for a bigger budget.

Both types of currency bought a new security operations center at the bank's headquarters. That's where Caroline parks the care package for her colleague, one of the new staffers she has hired to work there. Other new security employees, about 30 in all, have been hired or imported from New Jersey. Caroline keeps offices in both places.

In the security operations center, which they informally call the SOC, pronounced "sock," the security team quietly buzzes away. Stretching their legs and bumping their knees under their desks. Squinting and rubbing their eyes. Most of them are still getting used to all the natural light that the new SOC gets.

It's a move from the back office to the front office, at least that's what executives keep saying. From the back burner to the front burner. For some of the team members, it's an exciting change, getting noticed, coming to work at the corporate headquarters, where everyone dresses well and market-moving business decisions happen right under their noses. For others, it just feels like being on the burner.

The SOC has been over a year in the making. Everything was planned down to the last detail.

Inside the main room, which they call the secure room, 30 desks, each with four 20-inch widescreen monitors, are set up in a configuration they've tested on hackers in New Jersey to find just the right specs for left-right and up-down eye scanning. They look like this for each SOC employee:

Five 50-inch plasma screens span the east wall, one displaying scrubbed and fake data from an analytics software program called Splunk. The data is scrubbed or fake because the hackers working in the SOC, who are known officially as analysts, are deeply uncomfortable displaying real data on widescreen televisions. On the south wall, a 90-inch plasma screen plays CNBC on mute. Frances often watches it intently to see what they might be getting wrong.

The north wall is made up of 100 square feet of electrochromic glass. The analysts call this the fog wall. It has been constructed using a five-layer sandwich of ultra-thin glass and polymer layers, the middle layer being a separator with rows of thin, clear, invisible electrodes on either side. One of the layers is soaked in polycrystalline tungsten oxide. When someone flips a switch, lithium ions are attracted to one side of the sandwich, making the glass go white so it resembles a plain, opaque wall. Flip the switch again, and the glass goes clear, so you can see inside the SOC.

The fog wall is not meant as some kind of impermeable force field against cyberattacks, prying eyes, or malicious devices. It is meant to surprise and delight corporate clients who visit the bank.

The significant location, the fog wall, the blinking and blooping screens and high-tech computer setups serve one purpose: to entertain important clients coming through for a tour. Bankers talk to them in the sober confines of the walnut and forest-green atrium, then drop the lithium ion curtain and reveal those flashing, blinking plasma screens with their impressive graphics and all those young turks typing away feverishly on their keyboards. Keeping the financial sector safe from peril, live and in real time. That experience transforms a cost center into something more than what it is. Something *valuable*.

The fog wall faces an atrium on the twelfth floor of NOW Bank's headquarters, an area that previously served as a pass-through to get from one bank of elevators to another. The hallway includes a sitting area, outfitted in sober dark-wood furniture with tasteful, academic dark green accents.

On either side of the pass-through sits the company's global physical security team, which includes the people who issue credentials to employees and monitor bank robberies. Farther down the hall, there is a hair salon, a wellness center, a "mother's room" with three curtained stalls where nursing women pump breast milk throughout the day, conference rooms, a catering area, several meeting rooms, one fancy meeting room with soft couches, and lots of audiovisual equipment. Ensconced within these symbols of normalcy, the analysts inside the SOC prowl the bank's systems, waiting for an enemy to strike.

They will not have to wait long.

4.

The Baby

Ultimately, the SOC is about function, not style. The analysts in the SOC are good, probably some of the best in New York. They were hand-selected and hired by Caroline, after all. The bank itself is great at security. NOW Bank is great at security in large part because of all the writing, all the documentation, all the clearly outlined rules for employees, for letting people into buildings, for hiring and firing, all the rules for software security and rules for vendors and rules for budget projections and rules for intelligence reports. Their security posture on paper is outstanding.

Paperwork, maybe paradoxically, is frequently proven to be one of the best lines of defense.

Attacks are inevitable. The Defense Department sustains them daily, and the Defense Department is a war machine. A bank is not a war machine. It can't fight back, only defend. And even in that defense, the enterprise is constrained by the scenarios it has planned for. Those scenarios are recorded in the reams of paperwork. They are often theoretical, historical, or invisible—as in, nobody of significance will ever see that they happened—a fact that keeps the security function itself invisible.

That's why the DDoS attacks changed everything. Some executives have started to see the bank as a war machine. Some begin to view the bank as, at the very least, subject to a potentially high degree of embarrassment—called reputational risk in business speak—if it fails.

The cybersecurity staff got their chance to propose what they would do with a huge new budget. In response, Caroline and her team created one of the most ambitious series of PowerPoint budget proposals the world has ever seen. They asked for a lot of money and they got it. Many millions flowed into cybersecurity's budget. They built up the SOC. Better people came to work there. Paper wins again.

Then things took an unexpected turn, way out of the control of any of the people who did the work of cybersecurity. The bank's chief operations officer got his brother involved. Executives became obsessed with finding a marquee name to match the budget. Somebody who looked fantastic on paper, who had written books about cyberwar. Because they were a war machine now, right?

Enter Bob Raykoff.

There is a widely held view in the corporate world that luxurious, high-profile surroundings are necessary to keep the money flowing because money begets money.

But cybersecurity people, even the technical ones, don't need, nor do they necessarily like, expensive technology. Movies and television have misled their audiences on this point, because so much of what the analysts do involves sitting in chairs, eyes darting back and forth, calculating risks based on variables that constantly change. You don't need expensive accoutrements for that.

Impressive neon graphics and world maps with blinking lights

```
003e980: cde1 628c 515a 2cea 98e8 44d5 a18b 811b  ..b.QZ,...D.....
003e990: 5333 64be 22b0 1a2f de6f 68d7 81e0 5a0d  S3d."./.oh...Z.
003e9a0: 6f4f 4dc4 6b1a 62a4 1ddb 45aa 1e3f 3af8  oOM.k.b...E..?:.
003e9b0: 3dcd fc17 0b24 79b9 0225 9c1b c6ee 86a3  =...$y..%.....
003e9c0: 6e04 a551 f79f 1d06 fd3d 4b78 a430 376d  n..Q.....=Kx.07m
003e9d0: 6a3f 8616 d1f5 5469 468f 7a00 ae59 2af7  j?....TiF.z..Y*.
003e9e0: 70df cc71 ca66 c91c 8294 7e5d 38b5 23a8  p..q.f....~]8.#.
003e9f0: 6611 0d29 8c94 38cb 9090 8462 b728 2253  f..)..8....b.("S
003ea00: 27b9 3968 542d 809d 3b93 a33e 35c4 962b  '.9hT-..;..>5..+
003ea10: 2fdc d268 911d 6e80 13fc 24db 646b bc4e  /..h..n..$.dk.N
003ea20: 7796 24e0 d97a 4344 25cf 7ac9 25f8 eb4e  w.$..zCD%.z.%..N
003ea30: 20b1 46b5 fccf a99a 53b9 e227 277b a5d0  .F.....S..''(..
003ea40: 214f f3fa 8c13 7ec3 8d12 e6cd babe 8d24  !O....~.......&
003ea50: 1d2e 78f1 2560 2900 ec4a 2158 e2bf e7ab  ..x.%`)..J!X....
003ea60: 33fd 7b41 90f4 d14f 759e c199 cf19 5db0  3.(A...0u.....].
003ea70: 3d0f f77c c5ba ec31 94ab f34a a8d4 acad  =..|...1...J....
003ea80: d6bb a2f4 8126 c3bc ecba ce21 decb 0ba6  .....&.....!....
003ea90: 4417 77fb 3aad 80fb 548a 53cc 1649 45ea  D.w.:...T.S..IE.
003eaa0: fac7 c754 6cc0 db4a eb74 04aa 3247 1b98  ...T!..J.t..2G..
003eab0: 3c39 f467 fe32 f81a a733 c279 69ca 0cff  <.9.g.2...3.yi...
003eac0: a698 0a58 ca57 00ae 9d95 5233 925e 8953  ...X.W....R3.^.S
003ead0: c718 27c9 f7e0 9578 2e30 20c9 d6bc 1991  ..'....x.0 .....
003eae0: 1dcf d6de bc7e ffec c16d 13ca 7f4f 26c4  .....~...m...O&.
003eaf0: a515 a459 8041 ab67 84cd 23d0 7eff b7e4  ...Y.A.g..#.~...
003eb00: 1287 6d84 712c 7582 53a7 62f5 478b 0009  .m.q.u.S.b.G..
003eb10: be6b 3158 2cb0 fcdf 66e9 ea8b 4d4a fb94  .k1X,...f...MJ..
003eb20: 9334 0e91 d458 4e9b d03c 9202 691f d912  .4...XN..<..i...
003eb30: 72bb a549 824d 2e5a 5b61 ae36 dba8 a506  r..I.M.Z[a.6....
003eb40: cc44 8297 b558 bca1 a069 7e00 ea71 ccfc  .D...X...i~..q.
003eb50: f183 0e70 bce2 b709 61cb be2f ba8d c261  ...p.....a../...a
003eb60: 55a0 3b35 9751 ec04 cafe 9efb b8bf 75ec  U.;5.0.......u.
003eb70: 19c1 c939 5922 1d61 af52 8afa d1f1 fd1b  ..9Y".a.R......
003eb80: 599c 5d45 41c8 d8d9 1bba 6cb6 025c 1951  Y.]EA.....l..\.Q
003eb90: 35d6 bd26 4ea5 7d5c 0c53 bbe7 f5c4 da72  5..&N.}\.S.....r
003eba0: ea3e 1d94 391e 3dc6 f176 f440 00b9 d587  .>..9.=..v.@....
003ebb0: 3c5e 2b6d 40b8 91dd e923 9f55 f98e 32c2  <^+m@....#.U..2.
003ebc0: 78df b4b1 a6c0 ac35 fa25 be2f c675 31b4  x.....5.%./.u1.
003ebd0: 8795 ee58 0b65 d2c1 8cbc 35fc daa4 56f6  ...X.e....5...V.
003ebe0: 3434 f3e8 9f68 3b87 b1fb 7a81 f529 0fec  44...h..z...).
003ebf0: e972 98a7 f237 c589 cb79 77d9 00d5 b3fa  .r...7..yw.....
003ec00: ed73 6616 d130 42a6 8679 8030 df0f f9af  .sf..0B..y.0....
003ec10: d505 2a41 cdea bdd7 599c 31ab 61b6 ab89  ..*A...Y.1.a..
003ec20: 5627 13c7 a654 1526 67ee 281a 5285 2845  V'...T.&g.(.R.(E
003ec30: 6bd7 16d7 ed9d b930 4a26 327d 1324 0155  k....0J&2}.$.U
003ec40: 8911 274a 51ae de26 aad7 9114 ac51 5d6d  ..'JQ..&.....Q]m
003ec50: 5b5e baf3 d3f9 a94c eca0 5cf7 b3a6 6279  [^...L..\.....by
003ec60: 4a24 efc8 b221 89ef 5226 198f 79e8 0be5  J$...!.R&.y...
-- VISUAL LINE --                                    16025,1        49%
```

representing attacks are just a veneer, code on code. What most of the workers in the SOC see all day looks more like the above.

They also aren't terribly comfortable with being seen themselves. It quickly became a practical joke to flip the switch on the fog wall. Whenever this happened, rather than look out the clear glass, everyone simultaneously looked at the data on the plasma screens. They wanted to be sure nothing real incriminating was up there. Once safety was assured, then, perhaps, they would laugh.

Only a small handful of people truly care how the office looks, but it is one of Caroline's many jobs to care about this. The appearance of success and power confers actual success and power. Expensive art lines the walls of even the most modest meeting space. The bank displays Teddy Roosevelt's hunting rifle in a conference room on the fiftieth floor. The SOC is the cybersecurity equivalent of Teddy Roosevelt's hunting rifle.

You can't do good security without good security people, and really good, talented security people don't generally want to work in a bank. It costs money to rip them away from Silicon Valley, away from start-ups, away from Google and Apple.

There is no sign marking the SOC yet. The glass stays opaque most of the time. In order to enter the SOC, you have to know it's there. Then you need to notice the seam in the honey oak wall partition. That's the door, but there's no handle. There's a small electronic strip where you can swipe your security badge, but if you're not one of about 30 people out of 300,000 employees, you won't get access. So you have to knock on the wall.

On this day, as on most, Raykoff is nowhere to be found. His new office is in the reception area. It holds a row of six chairs and six desks in trader formation all facing south toward the floor-to-ceiling windows. It's so bright in there, the employees sometimes have trouble seeing their screens. There are usually only two people: a government relations person and the head of intelligence. They are support staff for the SOC. Government relations—a tall, angry Arab American ex-spook named Gabe who constantly drinks Red Bull—makes sure everyone from the FBI, NSA, DHS, branches of the military, and CIA feel like they are looped in. Gabe's job is to hold their hands and make sure they are invited to luncheons.

The head of intelligence, a quiet, brilliant Korean American ex-spook named Tom, takes all of the news and information feeds from the guys inside the SOC and turns it into a predictive report about what the next threat will be and where it will come from.

On this day, Caroline realizes she left her keys in the SOC. She sprints back, swipes her card four times to get back into the building, runs up the stairs, goes through security reception, and returns to the SOC, where she grabs her keys and quickly turns, glancing out the south-facing floor-to-ceiling windows. Sunlight floods the room and the view makes her catch her breath. It's so clear you can see all the way down Vanderbilt Avenue. She sighs. This place is her baby, too.

This is the house that nation-state hackers built.

In August 1994, a hacker named Vladimir Levin transferred $10 million, the equivalent of $250 million in 2018 dollars, via the telecommunications network to accounts in Sweden and Denmark. He had infiltrated the core banking components of the interbank wire system and intercepted communications channels between Citibank and the Depository Trust & Clearing Corporation, an intermediary that monitors and approves international wire transactions. It wasn't the first time somebody had stolen money from a bank using computers, but it was one of the biggest, most visible, and most highly publicized heists.

Citibank used a great deal of technology in 1995, but they had no cybersecurity department. They had a physical security staff. But the types of data breaches they'd dealt with in the past were more along the lines of an overturned truck on the New Jersey Turnpike that had been carrying data tapes to a storage facility.

The Levin incident would lead to the bank creating the first-ever chief information security office. The new department would help protect the bank's money. Not the data of its people, not the intellectual property or proprietary trading information. The money. Because back then, that's what people wanted to steal. Because they could. Russia allowed Levin to be extradited. He was later picked up at Heathrow Airport in London, flown to Manhattan, and sentenced to three years in jail for his crimes.

Hackers like Levin were 15 years ahead of the banks. Money is money, and when it's gone, it's gone. Citibank pumped funds into its new cybersecurity office, and other banks followed suit. In about a year, thefts of money directly out of bank coffers stopped almost completely.

Hackers had to find new things to steal in order to make money. It didn't mean they stopped targeting the banks, it just meant that they eventually gave up on trying to break into them and steal dollars. They turned to other things they could monetize, then to other types of companies that dealt in financial transactions, then to other types of companies, period. The practice of intercepting financial communications never ended, only the practice of specifically trying to intercept communications between banks and clearing houses. The targets changed but the tactics stayed the same.

Identities, bank account details, birth dates, credit card numbers, and maiden names became the new commodities. None of those things, of course, is money. When these things are stolen, they aren't really gone; they can be replaced. Because they are perceived as less valuable than money, it's harder to lock them down.

In May 2000, Vladimir Putin became president of Russia. The country had already established itself as one of the leading bastions of criminal hackers—like Levin—and one of the greatest sources of astonishingly gifted engineers and mathematicians. Those great engineers and mathematicians, builders of code, of cyberweapons, hackers of nation-states didn't associate with common criminals.

What they did was different. Many hackers, like the infamous German cyberoperatives who stole nuclear secrets from U.C. Berkeley computers in the 1980s, just went on to work desk jobs after their years of espionage.

But Putin saw the value in what hackers did, probably better than any other world leader. These criminals were incredibly sophisticated, some as much as the most gifted engineers, but they were messy and sloppy and weren't motivated by patriotism. They wanted money and power and women and respect. But Putin believed patriotism could be cultivated, especially if it meant gifted hackers would not get extradited, as Levin had, and their spoils turned into shared resources of the state.

Russia, both its government officials and certainly its criminals, turned its attention away from government assets in other nations and focused on business assets, which were poorly protected, if they were protected at all. Fewer and fewer cybercriminals were extradited. The state looked the other away when it came to taxing the hackers' illicit earnings. But when Putin came knocking at the door for a slice of the information stolen from U.S. citizens, cybercriminals knew they had no choice but to give it up. It didn't hurt their earnings and the state enjoyed the plausible deniability of being able to say it hadn't ordered anybody to hack anything.

On April 27, 2007, Russia attacked Estonia over a dispute involving an elaborate bronze statue of a Russian soldier in a Tallinn cemetery. To exact revenge for the removal of the war memorial, Russian criminal and state resources banded together and, most likely aided by a private-sector telecommunications company, took down a great many of Estonia's broadcast services and defaced many of its websites. This cyberwar, the first of its kind, would lead the North Atlantic

Treaty Organization to establish its cybersecurity headquarters in Tallinn. The decision was more than a symbolic gesture; today Estonia is a cybersecurity heavyweight.

But when Russia brought Estonia offline, it caught the attention of the world's militaries. And it emboldened young computer enthusiasts in Eastern Europe, especially Romania.

In 1994, when Vladimir Levin was stealing Citi's money, René Kreutz was born in her mother's bedroom in a communist bloc apartment in Arnica Valka, Romania. Mrs. Kreutz, a homemaker, and Mr. Kreutz, a police officer, had never seen a computer. They would give their daughter an abacus as a toy, in the hopes that she would take up mathematics. It would be the first thing she ever gripped in her tiny fist.

In 2000, when Vladimir Putin was sworn in as president of Russia, René saw a computer at a local library for the first time.

In 2007, the year René tried alcohol, she heard all about the Estonia attacks.

It was the Estonia event that made many of her young friends want to become hackers. Their motivation was half patriotic and half economic. Many of them hated the Russians for constantly using their digital might to assert themselves across borders. They also wanted to be rich and didn't see a way to get there through a traditional career. They didn't see themselves as criminals, just smart kids wanting to get one over on the world.

René would not follow in their footsteps, however. Computers didn't interest her. Math didn't interest her, to her parents' great disappointment. She liked to talk and wanted to be around people. It didn't mean she didn't respect the fevered pursuit of money or understand it, she just didn't take part. Some kids like soccer, some kids like dancing, and some like computers. René liked to party.

René's schoolmates were no different from other kids across Eastern Europe and Russia, especially former Soviet states. These kids were competitive, anarchic, and untethered from their countries or their governments. In many of these former Soviet nations, few resources were dedicated to legal enforcement of computer crimes. It was like an open invitation for hackers. They had the same mind-set as someone who dreamed of Silicon Valley or the dormitories of Stanford, but they lacked the opportunity to pursue a career in tech. So they created their own opportunities.

The competition to make money was fun for René's friends. It was unstructured. Online, they could match wits, swap techniques, and share code with Russians, Israelis, Iranians, Americans, Jews, Muslims, and Hindus. René thought it was more like World Cup soccer than cyberwarfare. This post-Soviet hacker culture solidified around a few ideals: making money is paramount; it's much more dignified to outwit opponents with a new innovation than to beat them with brute force; you need to show your country a little loyalty for letting you get away with this stuff.

By July 2014, while Caroline admires a perfect sunset in Manhattan, René is heading off to class. She is studying marketing. This class is on making PowerPoint presentations. She is boring her pants off at Arnica Community College. She sometimes wishes she'd paid more attention to what her friends were doing and gotten into computers, too. Many of them already had good jobs in Bucharest or Tallinn.

But she resigns herself to the work ahead. A marketing job will be nice. She dreams of being a spokeswoman for something, a professional talker. Something that involves being around people. She hates being online, despises social media, except to share pictures with her friends. She barely checks her email, never goes on Facebook. Prefers instead working her job as a waitress in the evening.

PowerPoint class is boring but there is still a certain art to it that she appreciates. She pours as much energy as she has into making her slides look perfect. She worries she is wasting her time because nobody ever made millions off nice-looking PowerPoints. Though hers are beautiful, there's no point in thinking that far ahead. There are hardly any businesses in Arnica Valka, or anywhere nearby, that need fancy PowerPoint presentations.

Bob Raykoff is lumbering his way around the SOC, introducing some important-looking businesspeople. According to some employees, his use of jargon from his prior position makes them uncomfortable and prone to distrust him.

Knowing glances have become currency in the SOC. Whenever Raykoff delivers a speech or tries to motivate them, the disconnection is so profound you can see the operators at their desks, completely motionless, only their eyes moving to meet with those of their deskmates. The unspoken message: "We're fucked."

Professionally, legally, even personally. Fucked because Raykoff is already bringing in second and third layers of executives from his pool of guvvy friends, people he knows well, an informant army of fall guys who will provide a cushion between him and the unpredictable staff.

Raising legitimate alarms up the corporate food chain will become harder, a huge problem in cybersecurity, as raw information will get filtered by the agendas of those in the middle before it reaches someone who can actually take action.

Raykoff goes back to his new office outside the SOC within earshot of a handful of employees. He logs onto his computer. Ten minutes later he is slamming the mouse down repeatedly. His administrative assistant enters the room.

"Everything OK?"

"Uh, ha." He grins sheepishly. "I can't get this thing to work."

"What is it you're trying to do?"

"Uh, this . . . onboarding training. For new employees." He sighs. "Honestly, I don't understand why someone in my position needs to do this."

"Let's have a look. You can't navigate through the training?"

She steps up behind him and takes the mouse. The training is on privacy obligations of security professionals. She clicks on the correct answer on the screen, five red Xs disappear, and the training module progresses. She smiles, pretending to not know that all she did was provide the correct answer to the question. A happy accident.

"There you go," she says, turning to leave the room.

"Wait a minute. Uh, I'm really slammed." He turns to his desk, shuffles a pile of papers for effect. "Could you finish this for me?" Pause. "This Home Depot thing's wild, right? Hopefully that's the worst thing we see this year."

She comes back to the desk. Glances at her colleagues standing outside the office. Currency is exchanged. She begins clicking through the correct answers, a tight smile on her face.

"No problem."

A short, muscular Israeli with Russian roots, Victor Tanninberg has all kinds of reasons why he can't hold down an office job. He despises authority. Can't stand working alongside other people. Hates answering questions. He has a PhD in string theory and sometimes can't be bothered to say what he is thinking out loud; it takes much longer than simply doing it. He doesn't do paperwork.

So 12 years ago, he put his PhD in string theory to work by learning how to program and tweak the electronic control units of GM cars. He has three cars, all modified. A navy blue Corvette and a black Crown Victoria with a Corvette engine. The Crown Victoria has a push bar and police spotlights. Then there is the dusty old Chevy Lumina that he lets his sister drive around.

The Crown Vic is a monster. It drives fast and turns on a pin and takes up far more space than it should. It is what he prefers to drive out to Padraigh's place in Newark. People tend to get out of his way when he drives the Crown Vic, which he appreciates.

Over those years, he's watched as the networks that operate those cars proliferate and grow to a degree that is similar to the interwoven, sometimes dysfunctional networks supporting NOW Bank. In Victor's case, the networks are made compact and introduce incredible complexity to each individual Malibu or Impala.

It's a job that's always challenging in some new way. A job that mostly always keeps him, blessedly, thankfully, out of contact with other people.

Now a reporter is bothering him. He hates reporters. The reporter is trying to get him to explain to her how car computers work and how they could be hacked. He explains, carefully, first that he is not a hacker. Then he describes how car computers have changed over the years to become more vulnerable. She treats Victor like he simultaneously represents every hacker, Russian and Israeli, who has ever lived.

"Have you heard anything about this breach at Home Depot?" she asks.

He hesitates. "No. From who?"

"From other hackers?"

"I am not a hacker, and I don't know other hackers," he says. Although, given his credit card issues, he wonders if it's related.

Victor knew the reporter from his post-academic career in the mid-2000s. Then, he was working in arbitrage. In traditional banking, this is the buying and selling of assets in different markets in order to make a profit off of price differences.

But Victor was no banker. And this arbitrage was not the type usually entertained by international financiers.

With a loosely connected group of physicists and mathematicians, he wrote code that took advantage of the growing popularity of online sports betting websites. He wrote bots that continuously parsed the sports betting sites to find arbs—combinations of bets on different websites weighted in such a way that a positive return is guaranteed regardless of which side wins. The ultimate hedge. Their work was landmark but completely under the radar. His group of friends eventually broke up, and he turned his attention to cars.

"So, let's get back to the cars. Why are cars so much more complicated today?" the reporter asks.

Victor speaks to what he knows of GM cars, and only the very basics. In the 1980s and before, cars were almost entirely mechanical. Electronics, in the form of computers, were introduced as engine control modules (ECMS) in the 1990s. Following that, the addition of powertrain and transmission control modules.

By 2006, GM had updated its on-board protocol, allowing for the proliferation of computers far beyond anything in the past, from two to fifteen or more: door-lock control, ABS computers, traction-control modules, and so on. After explaining the history of car computing, Victor has to remind the reporter once again that like most technologists, he's focused on only one part—the ECM.

Victor hates these questions. He only focuses on car performance, that's it. Anything nefarious is going to happen in those other control modules, and could be achieved only by someone with the desire to figure out how to work on and spread a nefarious action laterally across the whole network. A microcosm of a big bank, with all its loosely tied together parts. He wants to get the reporter off the phone before he can be bothered more.

People don't realize, he says, that if they do so much as get bigger tires on their car, the computer will be thrown out of whack. The speedometer will show that they are going 50 miles per hour when they are really going 60. And isn't that more dangerous on a regular basis, he says, than some hacker figuring out how to steal data from your infotainment system?

He hangs up, vaguely dissatisfied, feeling that the reporter didn't get the message. He gears up to go to work, out in the big, awful world today, much to his further disappointment.

Today, Victor's got a Camaro in Newark, N.J., that he needs to work on. His customer is Padraigh, who owns a repair shop for high-performance cars. He's doing fewer and fewer jobs like this these days, preferring to keep his business to mail order. He likes to be in the house, close to his son and his pet rabbit, but he's making a few final exceptions for his old friend.

At the performance shop, Victor sets cars up and runs them on a dynamometer, which measures functions like horsepower and torque. Using its readings, he'll tweak the software on the car's computer so that the car runs better. Some of Padraigh's customers drag race professionally, and they need to shift the gears on their Corvettes faster. These cars are their babies.

Victor, one of the world's best hackers of GM cars, whether he calls it that or not, doesn't worry about people hacking cars. He worries about his stolen credit card. He worries about the aging electrical grid. He is concerned about fearmongering by reporters. And especially about idiots who replace 16-inch wheels with 18-inch wheels without a care in the world.

5.

The Italians

It's sunny but cool for New York in late July in 2014. There's been a breach at NOW Bank. In the SOC, doors slam. Workers pull one another into empty conference rooms and whisper, looking both ways before closing the door. Eyes are wide as analysts share the gory details of what happened and how it happened, or how they think it happened.

Caroline is trying to manage the chaos, but first she has to find Bob Raykoff. Bob is missing, and he is needed in a meeting up here immediately. She sends word down to the second floor, where there are several conference rooms. He was supposed to make an appearance at a panel of chief investment officers but never showed.

She asks the conference staff to have someone look out for a tall, gray-haired man walking with purpose in wide circles around the conference floor. Ask for Mr. Raykoff. Just tell him he has a call on the twelfth floor. Caroline presumes he can find his office from there.

While Raykoff is MIA on the second floor, a new team member is moving into the SOC. Caroline is helping to prep him, too. Prem

Ramesh is now Raykoff's number two, in the newly created role of chief of staff. He wasn't the person Raykoff had wanted to hire. In fact, Prem had competed for Raykoff's job as the head of cybersecurity. Short, mid-30s, and sleek as a greyhound, Ramesh is nothing like his former rival and new boss. Instead, he was shoe-horned in as Raykoff's second in command and the leader of the bank's cybersecurity operations team.

Prem had built a consulting business within one of the country's biggest defense industrial companies and invented a framework for understanding IT security called the kill chain. It's been adopted not just by Raykoff and his compatriots but by many cybersecurity professionals as a simple way of describing how criminals commit cybercrime. It's a convenient soup-to-nuts narrative package for how a cyberattack works, from early reconnaissance to direct action by an attacker.

The philosophy behind it is simple: Interrupt the sequence at the earliest point in order to stop the attack and reduce the damage. Spend money to focus on finding criminals doing reconnaissance before they get all the way to command and control.

But for Prem's purposes, the lesson is more challenging because whoever has attacked NOW Bank is already on command and control.

Prem and a communications team are creating a PowerPoint presentation, sketching and resketching, trying to decide how to explain what they know about the intrusion so far in kill-chain terms.

First, it appears the criminals conducted significant research on the bank, reconnaissance at many different levels of the organization. They looked for personal details of employees on LinkedIn and explored the perimeter—the digital part of the bank that exists outside its firewalls—for ways in. They also researched other websites that may connect with the company. NOW Bank runs what is known as a flat network, which means that anyone who gains access to one part of the network can essentially access all of it, across all of those many organizations, all the way up to asset management, investment bank, and beyond.

The criminals take this valuable information and weaponize it. They use all of the data they have gathered to find a way in. They do a custom-made job for NOW Bank or for whoever else they may be targeting.

In one case, the criminals' research yielded two junior employees, contractors at a university program in Rhode Island, who were socially engineered to give up their credentials. Social engineering describes the variety of ways people can be convinced to give up sensitive information: whether through a clever email or a well-placed, convincing phone call. Sometimes a criminal will pose as a hapless technology worker trying to fix some problem for the target. It's called social engineering because the technique exploits your natural desire to trust another person; it essentially uses your politeness and willingness to help as a tool against you.

There is another area of entry that the reconnaissance also yielded: a half-marathon website for a yearly event sponsored by NOW Bank. The website itself was built by a third party, an outside public relations agency, at the behest of a discrete community service department within the bank. These types of projects can easily fall through the cracks. Since the race website was built insecurely but was allowed to connect to the bank's network in order to facilitate the sign-up of participants, anyone who could access the poorly defended race website could gain entry to the rest of the bank's vast network. Caroline and her team, and many security executives before her, had been advocating for network segmentation for years, a process that would have created drawbridges between various bank departments, but there was never enough funding.

It's therefore not much of a challenge for the criminals, who are clearly sophisticated, to deliver a weaponized bundle of malicious software to unsuspecting employees or through the unprotected website. The exploitation and installation portions of the kill chain involve using this conduit to execute the malicious bundle and install programs that allow the criminals to extract the information they want: in this case names, Social Security numbers, and other sensitive banking information belonging to NOW Bank customers who may be especially susceptible to a pushy stock scheme.

With this access now installed throughout the bank, the criminals are able to command and control their various malicious installations to forward all that sensitive information to their servers overseas.

NOW Bank is trying to determine which course of action to take. If they tip off the criminals that they are aware of their presence, it could cause them to take destructive action that could ruin the bank's servers and burn their trail. The attackers would do this only if they knew their nefarious activity had been discovered. So the SOC team has to work quickly and very quietly.

After three days of working on the kill-chain explainer, the cybersecurity team opts to destroy it before it's circulated further.

To continue working the incident quietly, the professionals in the SOC must try to determine what's being taken and which pipelines they will need to shut off to stop the problem.

There are many *other* problems that complicate this. First, the bank is using wildly different storage protocols from one department to the next. In a single organization, people in one department may have been saving their documents, reports, client lists, and other critical data to a database shared among similar employees, while in another department, people have the habit of storing these documents in duplicate to their email inboxes or on their desktops. These reports are given names, and those names would also be different across departments. Because of this, determining what is being taken is a monumental task in itself.

There are further complications. NOW Bank, like most large banks, has a patchwork-quilt network compromised by years of acquisitions. Different systems of storage and data layered on top of data and more data are a legacy hallmark of the 2008 financial crisis, when several failing banks were pushed together rapidly and haphazardly. Like those messy and fast mergers, the merged networks of those banks were equally messy, difficult to navigate, and difficult to secure, contributing yet more headaches for the cybersecurity staff.

In order to talk about the ongoing data breach as quietly as possible, the cybersecurity investigators give the incident a name: Venice. Apropos of nothing, the name is meant as a way to easily discuss what's happening with the breach in conversation without anyone, including the criminals, catching on to the use of language like "breach" or "intrusion." This way, the investigators can avoid tipping off the criminals who have taken up residence in their network.

Prem is speed-walking from one meeting to another to discuss Venice. Right now, the bulk of the conversations about the event are happening face-to-face to keep things quiet. Sometimes Raykoff is in the room, but most often he is not.

The focus on privacy will soon become more like an obsession, though. Because someone will start leaking details of the attack to the press.

About four weeks later, somewhere in what used to be called Transylvania, a German sits at a cafe by the highway, drinking strong coffee and reading *The Sydney Morning Herald*. The weather is hot and humidity is 100 percent, unlike the cool dry New York July.

Sig Himelman is a six-foot, four-inch hacker. He looks like a businessman. The waiter at the cafe treats him accordingly. Calls him boss. Comments on his good sunglasses.

His suit is crisp, dark navy seersucker, because it's hot this time of year in Romania and air-conditioning is hard to find. Leather shoes from a small, private shop in London. He's driving a black BMW, late model. He wants it to look like he bought it and has owned it for a long time. Practical. Not someone who needs to impress. Not someone who leases.

There's nothing in the paper that interests him. Nothing about Valery Romanov, at least not today. He had heard through the grapevine that Romanov had fired his lawyer. Again. Knowing what Sig knows about Romanov, America might not have enough lawyers to satisfy the man's ego. He picks up *The New York Times* and finds something that interests him—an article about something serious possibly happening at NOW Bank. Must have been a leak there. Tied to northern Italy, the paper says. He laughs. Ridiculous. Some Russians, Israelis, Chinese businessmen maybe. Northern Italy? Unlikely.

He contemplates briefly. Italy, if it was true at all, would just be a smokescreen. A server in Venice or Rome set up to receive pings from another server in Tel Aviv and a third in Beirut, a fourth in Japan.

"What's so funny, boss?" the waiter asks as he takes a seat at the table next to Sig.

"Italians. Reporters."

"You Italian?"

"Yes." He says it without hesitation.

"I thought you were German. Your accent is very German."

"I had a German uncle who taught me English." Another easy lie.

"You're not a reporter, too?"

Sig laughs, raises his sunglasses to his head. "Of course not."

"Reporters, they always lie, no?"

"I don't think it is that they lie. No, no," Sig says, settling into his chair. He spreads his arms wide and knits his fingers together behind his head, a gesture of expansive command of the environment. "They are like teenage boys watching pornography. They look and say, '*See, they are fucking! Now, she's had an orgasm! Look!*'"

The waiter laughs and sips his coffee.

"And in five minutes they are finished. They think they have witnessed the act of sex, that they could describe it to someone else. But they cannot. They see only what the actors and producers and cameraman and Viagra maker and plastic surgeon want them to see. And they talk about the long hairless legs, the perfect fake tits, then they drink beers together and congratulate themselves for being experts on fucking."

Everything is an illusion. Sig hasn't hacked a computer in a decade but is regarded as an influential hacker. He has never worn a hooded sweatshirt in his life. He may have a personality disorder, but he definitely doesn't have emotional problems. He doesn't need a therapist like this American Mr. Robot. He does not suffer from depression. He does not lack for friends or female company. He is never awkward, but as smooth and soft and familiar as his gently worn leather BMW seats.

Today, he is headed to a new job in a village near Arnica Valka. He already knows a lot of carders who work there, many of whom have made money off Romanov's instruction and processes. Some of them are very good. He wants to pull them into a more cohesive unit, and they want the same thing. Some people are amenable to having a boss. Start-ups need CEOs. Even criminal ones.

Germany is becoming a surveillance state, he thinks. He traces over a story about the BaFin, Germany's financial regulator, buried on the back page of the B section. Something about them coming down hard on Deutsche Bank for bad culture. He has insiders at Deutsche Bank. *Bad culture.* Oh, they have no idea.

BaFin, Sig had real problems with. Regulate this, regulate that, squeeze all the fun and ingenuity out of the entrepreneurial process. Root out insider threats. Give power to whistleblowers. But one man's insider threat is another man's whistleblower. Surveil them all!

Criminals are ahead of everyone. He pulls out another Australian paper.

"Newspapers," the waiter says. "I see you like the newspapers. Newspapers are good. Everyone today with the iPhones."

"I guess I'm just paranoid. Don't want to be tracked." Sig smiles. An infectious smile, one that leads to the eyes.

"They can do that, you know. That's what I've heard." The waiter's voice is a low whisper. "The *Russians.*"

"Oh, well, what can you do? I'm not really into these things. I like the feel of the paper on my fingers." A bigger smile. He orders a slice of spinach and cheese pie and turns back to his reading.

He bought the papers on his commute from Hamburg. He's been reading nonstop about the burgeoning market for a new kind of financial instrument: ransomware. Malware that locks up a person's files and generates an encrypted key that the person must then buy in order to access their own files. He's trying to gauge how it's perceived in the real world.

It is a flawless business proposition, he believes. The world is filled with little law firms and consulting firms and one-man shops that need to work every day, every hour, gears constantly grinding. They will pay the $500 to get back to work if the gears stop, especially when their yearly revenue is in the millions. They can pay this modest sum again and again, all over the world.

Ransomware is new, and has been percolating quietly, below the surface, for about a year. He hasn't yet figured out the best way to monetize it. But the market for carding is changing, becoming too crowded, too boring. The fact that Russia allowed Romanov to get extradited proved that whatever the big carders were doing is no longer important, that carding itself is no longer important. And Sig likes to be important.

A widespread ransomware attack had hit media outlets and the Australia Post, a national mail courier based in Melbourne. So of course, they are reporting on it. Inside the second paper is a screenshot of a PowerPoint slide from the ransomware attackers. Sig studies it—green text on a black background. It is spare, rife with misspellings, ugly. "Once you've paid, than you can have your files back," it reads. Sig shakes his head. Hackers can be so inelegant.

The newspaper doesn't say whether the Post paid the ransom, which he assumes means they have. Imagine how much more they might have paid if they thought they were dealing with a serious criminal enterprise? Not some foreign kids who don't know the difference between "then" and "than."

Sig sets down the newspaper. Gets out a napkin. Asks the waiter for a pen. Begins to sketch out a plan for a ransomware business.

Sig is deeply interested in the concept of criminal organizations as business organizations. And as cybercrime goes, it can be one of the most challenging problems to overcome in turning a profit. Imagine a version of any American office, include all the drudgery, paperwork, sniping, and backstabbing, but add to it an entire workforce made up of people with a very loose relationship with the law, and subtract much of the face-to-face interaction.

Sig appreciates the advantages organized cybercrime has over traditional, Mafia-based organized crime. First, there are hardly any laws that robustly prohibit the kinds of crimes they will be committing. This is especially true in the countries of Eastern Europe. It's not necessary to involve oneself in the messy business of bribing police or prosecutors when nobody's looking for you.

Second, there is more churn and more opportunities for small, independent criminal groups to form. For those few big shots, like Valery Romanov, who happen to be incarcerated, their ability to run a criminal enterprise ends. That's because their access to computers is shut off, and unlike the old-school mafiosi, they can't conduct their business merely by prison phone.

This means new leaders can take their place. Sig is hoping he's among them because, unlike the Mafia, these individuals don't need to come from the same family.

Sig also knows a fair number of ex-criminals who went on to do legitimate work, especially after they did time in prison.

In Sig's experience, hacking collectives typically resemble start-up businesses more than old-school mafiosi. Divisions of the organization are best left to specific talent classes. Some specialists in arcane, difficult technology disciplines may work autonomously, and hiring them comes at a premium.

In bigger organizations, there are even human resources functions and customer service divisions. Some groups also have cybersecurity divisions of their own, which keep other criminal groups from stealing the illicit intellectual property they are creating and stealing.

Sig loves start-up culture. This is what he seeks to emulate. The new organization he hopes to build will include intelligence specialists to collect reconnaissance and a malware specialist—whom he knows from experience—to help design or alter existing components. He'll also use specialists who can deliver, exploit, and install the malware on the targets. Guys who are good at operating command and control servers and directing botnets, or large collections of compromised computers and devices.

Once he's got these pieces in place, Sig will set up a collections department to make sure people pay up. This collections person will be proficient in various clandestine money transfer methods and cryptocurrencies, to facilitate ransom payments from a global series of victims.

Most of the people he has in mind are men in their 20s to 40s from around Eastern Europe.

Finally, he wants a customer service rep. A pretty girl. Someone to temporarily offset all the testosterone that, he knows from experience, will ultimately break the organization apart.

That shouldn't be too difficult, Sig thinks. He's never had a problem getting the attention of an attractive woman.

Caroline is trying to organize her thoughts. She is pregnant with her second child and she can see the writing on the wall—Raykoff's new organization has no place for someone like her, someone who knows and is friendly with everyone, who is well loved and plugged into many cybersecurity communities. She is, in a word, dangerous.

The breach has slowed many things down, so news of her pregnancy came later than she would have liked. But the conversation with Raykoff was still jarring. She told him about her pregnancy, let him know when she would be taking maternity leave, approximately six months away now. It's considered polite protocol to not let something like a baby's arrival sneak up on your boss, and Caroline is congenitally on the right side of protocol. His response was predictable but cast a pall over her nonetheless: "When you get back from leave, you won't have a job in cybersecurity anymore."

Not "you won't be working for me," or "you won't be working in my division," or "you won't be working in this company." "You won't have a job in *cybersecurity* anymore." The threat was specific. She felt like he intended to blackball her. Her solace was that although he may have had the power to do this when he worked in government, he did not have the same power over the finance sector.

Still, his reaction has thrown her off. She has been seeking consolation from her vast network of peers. They have her back, as she always had theirs. They are enraged about this turn of events, even more than she is.

Now she sits with Michael Joseph, a former Marine Corps drill sergeant who is one of her closest confidants, and one of her earliest hires. He is filling her in on details of Venice. It's a Sunday night. Everyone has lost track of time. Their conversation is scored by the sound of quiet typing inside the SOC.

The security analysts detected the trip wire set by the attackers and have observed several terabytes being exfiltrated—taken out of the bank—all by the same perpetrator. As part of the investigation, they have found other problems, other attacks, other exfiltrations. They don't know yet how much data has been taken or what was in the data. It will be a very long time before they find out who did it. Possibly never.

Raykoff had been going around telling every executive who will listen that this is war. It looks like Chinese influence, he says. Game-changing, he says.

Michael agrees. It is big. And different. Not the sort of thing they have been trained for. They are a team of technologists first, engineers who understand protocols, controls, wonky stuff meant to create a relatively safe-as-possible environment. Michael has spent time on the battlefield in Afghanistan, but that was different. Banks don't go to war with the enemy, Marines do. When the enemy attacks a bank, Marines step in to control the situation. But there are no troops on the ground here. No NSA. No DHS. The FBI has been in touch, but not to do battle, to help figure out who is behind Venice.

The bank wants to both cooperate politely with and keep the three-letter agencies at bay, as most companies do if they can help it. Keep them vaguely satisfied and cordoned into their own investigative corners. The more agencies, the more leaks. The more agents, the more leakers. And the agencies didn't have the cyberarmy to help the bank anyway. They simply aren't set up to deal with cyberattacks spread out across every company in the country, each with its own internal politics and lingo and an unwillingness to share information with the government.

Then there's Raykoff. He knows something about the current threat. He understands how kinetic warfare can be executed. He understands the threats.

True, he might not have the depth of knowledge about the most current technical landscape. But that isn't the real problem. The real problem is that, based on his lack of experience in the finance sector and based on his early interactions with bankers, he doesn't appear to have a good grasp of how a bank works. He doesn't seem to understand that bankers are unlikely to listen to him since he's coming from a cost center, and pounding the table won't change their minds. His connections to the Pentagon no longer matter. Instead of focusing on how to explain what is happening with the breach to his counterparts across the bank, he defaults to Cold War rhetoric and sends frightening emails to employees who might leak to media, which is apparently what happened.

Michael slaps his forehead. "Did you see the article?"

"What article?" Caroline is too depressed to read the news, even about NOW Bank.

He pulls up a *New York Times* piece on the breach. An obvious leak from within. Some details of the attack are completely on point, others are totally wrong. One sticks out as being particularly egregious. The reporter says that sources inside the firm say the attack likely originated in northern Italy. They laugh. Italy isn't known as a hotbed of malicious activity. It is dead wrong. It's Russia, maybe Israel, possibly China.

Reporters are terrible at telling stories about cybersecurity. The hushed, striking mystery in the writing belies the clunky reality behind the scenes. Michael and Caroline go over the details again, trying to figure out who could have leaked the story. Who could have gotten a detail like that so wrong?

Then Caroline looks up, as if she could see the interaction unfolding in front of her. A confused, nervous internal source. A reporter with no grasp of the subject matter.

"*They're calling it Venice.*"

They both laugh out loud, disturbing some of the SOC workers.

It's 9 p.m. on a Sunday. Somebody knocks on the door.

Prem speed-walks inside. "Dinner's here!"

The sound of typing finally stops.

6.

The Gig Economy

Three months have passed. In Romania, things are going well with Sig's new company, which he has decided to call TechSolu. It's a nonsense term that simply sounds like an Eastern European tech start-up. He stole the logo from a manufacturer of vacuum cleaners. It's a half sun. Not that it matters.

He creates a meager website describing the company as an IT security service provider and leaves it at that. He manages to hire 10 new employees, all men—boys really—two of them from Poland, one from Russia, the rest from Romania. It is good to have a little diversity, he jokes to his new colleagues, referring to the Poles.

But Sig wants a woman in the office, too. Women keep everyone calm. Things get weird in an office with all men. People steal things. They fight, say racist things. They talk about sex too much, and if they're not talking about it, they're thinking about it. They steal intellectual property. Adding at least one woman creates a civil dance. It's not a perfect solution, but it is a form of risk mitigation.

They have been piecing together ransomware, bought from a variety of kits available on the dark web. It works well.

At the beginning, it was just Sig and the Russian, whose name is Mikael Gunther. Before coming to TechSolu, he had been fiercely independent. He had partnered with a Chinese hacker who was also inclined to solitude.

Together they ransomed grandmothers for their grandkids' photos, locking them up and asking for $50 or $100 to unlock them with the proper code. The grandmas never suspected what was happening was even a crime, as Gunther made it appear to be some sort of exploitative part of the Windows operating system. They are ethical—they asked the grandmas for their credit card numbers but didn't steal the numbers, only took the ransom payment. That's what Sig likes about Gunther. He is an ethical criminal, someone he can trust, at least a little bit.

Gunther reengineered the exploit kit and ultimately sold it on the dark web, cutting out his Chinese partner. He made more money selling the kit to other would-be ransomers than he would doing the ransoming himself. Gunther's toolkit was exceptional. That's how Sig found him.

They build a more enterprise-worthy version of Gunther's model, and that helps jump-start their business through trial and error on small law firms with lucrative clients. It is a relief to Gunther, who finds working with contacts in China to be exhausting.

Chinese, Gunther tells Sig, prefer a smash-and-grab way of doing things. It is antithetical to the Russian approach to hacking, which must always involve some level of stealth. It's just no fun without the intrigue, he says.

To illustrate this, Gunther talks disparagingly of his Chinese former colleague, who eventually changed his model to a pay-to-play arrangement. The last he'd heard, the partner had tried to get a job consulting with American companies concerned about security at their Asian branches. Gunther scoffs at this. "Sellout," he says.

Gunther helps Sig bring in other people from his network. Some come to sit with them in Arnica Valka, while others work remotely. The village itself is slowly becoming a destination for criminal hackers. There are many such pockets throughout Eastern Europe, but how many could boast the scenic countryside of Transylvania? A steady stream of curious specialists keep turning up in Arnica Valka. But only a handful of the townies seem to grasp what is going on.

With his first 10 employees, Sig puts the focus on targeting law firms and consulting firms. The reconnaissance on these is almost scandalously easy. Law firms in particular like to brag about their acquisition of new celebrity clients or their representation of large companies in a merger or acquisition. They send out a press release, swell with pride about it all over LinkedIn, write a pitch article about it for some trade magazine. Press releases provide the information necessary for the easiest and most obvious lures.

Gunther and the team at TechSolu find the firms quickly. In a typical ransomware pass, they execute a well-crafted email that appears to be a congratulatory note to one attorney from a colleague at another firm, based on whatever news was posted.

The note includes a link that, when clicked, allows TechSolu to deploy ransomware onto the machines of the law firm partners, locking them up. Then a frightening-looking green screen appears telling the attorneys that to get back access to their files, they need to pay a ransom of $500 to $5,000, depending on what the law firm can likely afford. That number is based on TechSolu's intelligence gathering.

Rival ransomers are sending out scattershot emails. Rivals aren't always unlocking the files after collecting the ransom.

But Sig knows the importance of building up a rock-solid reputation for reliability. This is a start-up, after all. He wants TechSolu to become known among victimized companies as an honest criminal organization, one that their insurance companies will be comfortable with.

This is especially important because now some insurance policies are starting to reimburse law firms for the ransom. If the insurance company is assured that the firm will get its files back in exchange for the ransom payment, they will approve it. And they do, and Sig and his compatriots get paid. And paid well. As their reputation for honesty in these transactions grows, so does their ability to collect higher amounts.

He still needs to find a woman.

Most of their victims require a great deal of convincing to pay up, and the lousy green screen with its dire warnings doesn't always do the trick. And nobody in the office speaks English as well as Sig. Sometimes the victims need to ask simple questions: "How do I set up a Bitcoin wallet?" Or "Are you able to read the files that you stole?"

Sig's answer to the last question differs, depending on the company. Because some of these law firms have more interesting information than others. Future mergers. Pending bankruptcies. The answer is always "yes," but usually he tells them "no" just to keep the transaction moving and pockets the valuable information for later.

Truthfully, Sig hates answering questions. He recognizes that a throwaway phone line with a dedicated customer service representative will go a long way in getting more payments through and increasing the organization's cachet among victims.

Not victims. Clients. "Clients" sounds much better.

There is another angle. A third TechSolu employee, Jakub Brik, stands out as the only African in the bunch, Polish only by way of Nigeria. He has become quite good at consulting. For the very small businesses, he is able to talk them through the process that will ensure they don't suffer another ransomware attack.

These small businesses often pay up gratefully at the end of the conversation. Jakub's consulting is further legitimizing the business, perhaps even enough so that Sig can hire somebody wholly legitimate. One of the pretty waitresses from the restaurant downtown, maybe.

Caroline hired Charlie Mack. Although he's a lawyer and was technically brought on by NOW Bank's legal department, it was her connections who got the ex–CIA officer and Harvard lawyer into the bank to oversee all of their cybersecurity troubles from a legal point of view.

What Caroline knows and a few select others suspect is that Charlie Mack is a goddamn hero. He's a corporate lawyer now, sure, but he's a legend and a bona fide hero. He never brings it up. Just thinks about it sometimes when some executive tries throwing a bad lawyer joke at him. *Listen to me, asshole, I'm trying to protect you from yourself. I was raiding Gaddafi's compound just last year. Do you think I'm being overly fucking careful?*

It is helpful to have a guy like Charlie around for crises, and Venice is going to be a big one.

But there are at least two others brewing at the bank. The first involves some of the bank's law firms. Chinese nationals have been stealing proprietary data on deals for years in order to insider trade. It's getting worse. They're starting to share that information with other operatives in other countries. Hundreds of them. Insider trades galore. The Department of Justice is investigating. The Securities and Exchange Commission is investigating. But the law firms are clueless.

Then the SEC was hacked, too, by the same people. The cycle continues.

The Chinese are out there smashing and grabbing and they've got their mitts on some heady stuff. They treat hacking like a full-time job, a cushy military career, a nine-to-five with on-the-job training. Imagine if safecracking were institutionalized, what would the safecrackers do when they retire? Take up fishing? Not when they can make much more doing the same thing underground.

Many of the attacks, workers in the SOC now know because of some public intelligence reports they've received, originate from a gray cement building in Shanghai known as People's Liberation Army Unit 61398. It's a sooty place where employees of China's PLA cyberunit have been hacking U.S. corporations for their intellectual property since at least the early 2000s. In the SOC in New York, the security analysts record electronic pings from the facility throughout the Chinese workday. They see a reprieve only on Chinese holidays.

The Chinese use rudimentary toolkits to break the meager defenses at most U.S. companies and steal swaths of data, most of it useless. Business plans, names of partners, dates, images, corporate charters, movies, embarrassing and incriminating information like names of mistresses and favorite kinks. They are especially interested in visiting businessmen.

Two Chinese schemes running simultaneously involve information from NOW Bank and some of its competitors, data that has been mishandled terribly by their respective law firms. Both schemes concern initial public offerings.

These two law firms deal in data related to mergers, acquisitions, and financing. Some of their divisions also handle Food and Drug Administration approvals and loans for pharmaceutical companies.

NOW Bank helps finance these deals, so the information resides with them, but their law firms have access to it as well.

Knowing that an unannounced merger is going to take place or that a drug trial was successful is a great way to get key information in order to execute an insider trade. The term "insider trading" used to refer to corporate insiders, company leaders, nosy bankers, and Wall Street journalists using their access to exploit the markets. But the new insiders are hackers who plunder corporate networks, and they are making hundreds of millions.

These guys get all the benefits of insider trading without having to ever rub shoulders with bankers, lawyers, or government officials.

Luckiest fucks in the world, Charlie says, just to make Caroline laugh.

It's now October 2014. Six years earlier, Bolin "Bo" Chou, a bisexual Shanghai expat from a village near the Nepalese border, learned how to create fake credit cards from a younger, less cynical Valery Romanov. This was in the spare time he had away from his job at PLA 61398.

Bo doesn't like talking about his government work. Not because it is supposed to be secretive. It is. But that's not the reason.

It's boring. A boring story. Strapping in, executing code all day, reworking old hashes, trudging home, filling quotas. He likes computer engineering and is pretty good at it. He loves data and what it can do. He is interested in how hackers in other countries operate. White hats and black hats. They are all the same to Bo.

Because what is he? He is good, he wears a white hat, he is fulfilling his duty to country. He is bad, he wears a black hat, he is doing things that are illegal in other countries.

People like Valery Romanov, they probably think they are white hats, too, when everyone else thinks they are pure black. Everything and everyone, all over the world, is gray, in Bo's opinion.

He loves Valery Romanov, not because he admires him, but because Romanov is pure camp. Romanov, the Russian rock star. Romanov, who posts pictures of himself with stacks of money and fancy cars. Romanov, who identifies with American rappers and calls himself Tupac. It was all so much flashier than Bo's work at PLA 61398.

Valery is fun and ultra-capitalist with a persona much bigger than anyone working in a Chinese hack farm could ever dream of. Bo doesn't want to emulate him, mind you. Just enjoy the show. He got into rap because of Romanov. Biggie, Tupac.

Then Romanov disappeared.

Then, it turns out, Romanov got arrested.

Bo, out of the army for a few years now, considers a different career.

In the tech-heavy suburbs of Shanghai, he tries getting into the skin care business for a while, selling pearl lotion to tourists. He moonlights as a tour guide, taking foreigners on tours of factories that make those pearl-based skin care products. He thinks about starting his own line of moisturizers. Then he gets a job washing dishes at one of the fancy hotels near the convention centers. And everything changes again.

Turns out, he loves the excitement of the hotels, the hustle and bustle. It's all new, fun, sexy to him. It is the polar opposite of the military job. It is different, too, from the cynical, clandestine world of the Russians and newbie cybercriminals and hackers and DEFCON wannabes he'd gotten to know online. It is better than the "hacker community," whatever that means.

Everything else has changed, too. Bo is bi, and he likes to be quiet about that. He'd joined the army and moved to Shanghai in the first place to get away from the traditions of his home life farther west. Traditions with no room for his ambiguous preferences.

Bo thinks the visionary European and American businessmen and -women are attractive and interesting. The Israelis, wily and clever. Even the Australians and Canadians are elegant and sophisticated in their own ways, with their bold and contagious friendliness.

And here he is, struggling with his identity as part of the Chinese contingent of the world's most boring hackers. Really, more like hammers, brute-force pounding away over and over and over again at infrastructure in the English-speaking world. Pound, smash, grab the pieces, pound, smash, grab the pieces, pound, smash, grab the pieces. Then screech out of there on worn-out tires, so everyone in the neighborhood can hear.

So Bo stays at the hotel job. Gives up the skin care tours in favor of a better racket. He rises to the status of lead doorman, because he can speak English well and remembers every detail about every guest. A nice rollover habit from his army days doing cyber-reconnaissance. He greets taxicabs, takes bags to rooms, helps direct the elegant businessmen and savvy businesswomen to the best restaurants, tailors, plastic surgeons.

At around the same time Charlie Mack is contemplating the mess in front of him at NOW Bank, Bo discovers even more reasons to love his new job, reasons that promise a beautiful marriage of past and present.

Bo is planning a fascinating evening of cyber-reconnaissance when he is distracted by a harried businessman who has left a satchel with his passport in it in a taxicab that is disappearing out of the hotel's circular drive.

The taxi driver isn't paying attention, and screeches out of the driveway. Bo takes off down the road. Running at a full clip for at least a quarter mile. Flat out. Like Jason Fucking Bourne, but in a black suit with a mandarin collar. He catches the taxi as it pulls up to a stoplight and pounds on the door. He manages to open it and jumps inside even as the driver tries to ignore him.

He demands the taxi driver turn around and go back to the hotel. The driver is irritated he has to travel with a passenger without getting paid. Bo promises him he'll get paid. Bo arrives back at the hotel, and the driver continues ranting and raving out the window. Bo tips the driver extra knowing that getting the American's passport back is the bigger win.

The businessman is pleased, of course. He tries to tip Bo for his trouble, but with a series of bows, Bo conveys that it is his honor to help the guest and that, if he likes, the guest should send a laudatory note to the hotel's manager. Bo is a master of keeping his stock in his primary employment high—a necessity, if he wants to keep his side gigs.

Bo wants nothing else from this guy. Did you suspect something insidious? Bo would blush to say it out loud, but he is a firm believer in the mantra of don't shit where you eat. He leaves the patrons of his own hotel alone.

But he hacks everyone else. Not in some blunt-force *Chinese* way, or for terrible nation-state reasons, but smoothly, elegantly, like an Israeli would or a good Russian who didn't care for money like Romanov did. He is never the *best* hacker. He always tries to be the most stylish, though.

Carding really isn't for him, too illicit. The Eastern Europeans, with their criminal groups and rules and business structures, are getting too aggressive and difficult to work with from afar.

Since it is data that he loves, he focuses on that. He is obsessive about it, collating it, parsing it, making it look gorgeous. Data is useless without someone with the skills to make sense of it, and the industriousness to do so is rare. He knows he has a niche. Data has become a valuable commodity, *the* commodity, more valuable than credit card numbers if you know how to present it right.

Every big company says so. Some companies, he knows, like Facebook, are already successfully making money off of it. He can see it on the back end. But what the general public doesn't seem to realize is that all of that data is essentially useless. Unless you care about stuff like politics and elections. And Bo does not. Too vulgar.

So Bo has begun working the travelers to the Shanghai convention center for information alongside his hotel gig.

It is exciting, and every week there are new industries—home improvement, medical devices, housewares, paint, computers. The list goes on and on. Financial firms. Nonprofits and NGOs.

The people attending are international business experts, perfect targets. He uses a commonly available type of malware that can help him get as much information on a company as quickly as possible. He delivers it through USB devices that he scatters around the convention center, making it easy for unwitting professionals to pick up and stick right into their computers, computers with all those spreadsheets and proprietary client lists.

Bo finds a great, cheap supplier from down south who sells him thousands of USB storage devices for around $100. One Monday morning, he goes down to the area that sells lots of mass-produced tchotchkes and buys a few beautiful, polished, modern-looking silver bowls.

Then Bo loads malware on each device. He creates a very professional-looking sign, one that mimics whoever is sponsoring the convention in color and font, and puts the USB devices in the beautiful silver bowl. "Free USB Storage. Welcome guests!" He leaves them, surreptitiously, in the lobbies of the hotels or the convention center cafeteria or, if he can slip in, its press room, where all the media outlets take their breaks and meetings.

In the early days of this scheme, convention-goers would pick up the devices and use them much more frequently than they do today. Many people have learned such freebies might be risky, and Bo is fine with that. Because the ones who pick them up are enough. He isn't greedy.

Once the simple malware loaded onto the USB drives is installed onto their computers, Bo grabs as many spreadsheets—just spreadsheets—as he can from their machines. The malware will probably be caught in a routine scan by some corporate technology team when the travelers get back to New York or San Francisco or London or Brisbane, but by then it will be too late. Bo will have everything he needs, including all of the emails and personal details of the individual's business contacts. He particularly likes getting business plans, budgets, future merger ideas.

Then, after all this excitement, the denouement. What does Bo do with this valuable information? He has an account on Fiverr, a legitimate, U.S.-based website for freelancers, and he sells this business intelligence to other companies. Companies that love the breadth and depth of his data but have no idea where it came from and know better than to ask.

The platform behind Fiverr is fairly simple. The baseline price is $5, which is where anyone using it to sell goods starts. Bo picks a simple interface, lists his location as Japan, uses a special program and a virtual private network (VPN)—a program that masks his movements from the Chinese government. To an outside observer, it would look like Bo's computer is pinging from a Tokyo apartment complex.

From there, he offers "curated" lists made up of "publicly available" corporate information on big players in all the industries that have trade shows in Shanghai. Building materials. Finance. Risk and compliance. Even money laundering. He starts with a $5 price tag for a basic report.

Of course, his intel is so good, the business quickly grows. And he is so good at curating it, business contacts recommend him to others in their industry. He becomes especially popular with salesmen looking for detailed prospect lists. He becomes a master at PowerPoint, making the data even more digestible to his less-than-tech-savvy customers.

The platform helps him get paid in all kinds of currencies—U.S. dollars, euros, cryptos—all of which are far more valuable than his local currency.

But even this is wearing thin. Bo wants to go legit permanently. His love of the business-class lifestyle means he is starting to find the pursuit of illicit gains to be far too vulgar. The problem, of course, is the scheme is so lucrative and so easy he can't afford to give it up.

7.

The Tryout

Caroline is preparing for a hack-a-thon. It is meant to get young engineers to come to the bank and showcase their skills.

It is an all-night affair. Coding through the wee hours of the night. The kind of opportunity that younger people, seeing promise in working at a bank, might jump at.

They are all college students, a few still in high school. Caroline will put them through their paces, allow them to write new code to fix a variety of problems. She gathers some of the engineers into teams to allow them to maliciously hack one another on a fake bank network.

It is billed as a charity event, but it is really a tryout camp.

Caroline makes sure the results are meticulously recorded. Early on in events like this, one or two rock stars are always evident. Kids who just have it. Perfect 10s.

And she likes to pull those people out of the crowd. Sit them down for a tea. Talk to them about how important cybersecurity is to the financial services sector. How rewarding it is to come work as a hacker for a bank. The bonuses they can make. The importance of a prestigious, marquee name on their resumes. A name like NOW Bank.

But today, despite the excitement of what's to come, she is really tired and really pregnant. She is a short, petite woman, and being really pregnant is no joke. It means serious balance issues. It means almost constant trips to the bathroom. And to her, it means worrying about her job because it seems like women in the department run by Bob Raykoff are being "managed out." That is the euphemism in corporate speak for an unspoken but established technique of making one's work life so unpleasant and unrewarding that one will want to resign voluntarily, thus saving the company severance pay and possible litigation. In her opinion, Bob is a jerk, but not of an outstanding type. This is a standard work challenge, endured by women all over the world, one she's helped many of her employees through and one she intends to weather with dignity.

But it's hard. The sighs and wan smiles from people who know she's not coming back from maternity leave wear her down. So do the congratulations, both parties understanding that she's just forfeited her bonus for the year. This is Caroline's second time through this, which is a blessing and a curse. When it's your first baby, everyone around recalibrates their expectations because they know your loyalties are going to be split in a most significant way. *How will she make my project her priority with a baby to worry about?* God, she hated that.

She's comforted because she has her network to lean on. Her former boss, Joe, the Kool-Aid Man, has moved on to a job at an insurance company. Nice and safe out in central New Jersey.

Another of her charges, Frances, the woman she prepared a care package for when her house burned down, gets Caroline an offer from a consulting firm. It would be a huge raise. She turns it down, knowing that what she wants next is something a little quieter.

She tries to tell the kids at the hack-a-thons that the trope of a morally tormented genius like Mr. Robot couldn't be further from the truth. Most people in this field are just normal, average Joes. Some are even mom types, sitting there, organizing the program, making sure everyone's on time and under budget. Getting into the field and getting good at it won't make you cool if you weren't cool to begin with. And that's OK. Cool people are frequently unreliable.

When Caroline had her first child, she was 35. She's now almost 40. Just before giving birth that first time, her doctors discovered a significant and possibly deadly tumor on her thyroid. She brought the baby, a boy, to term, underwent a C-section, and then immediately went into surgery to have her tumor removed on the same day.

She endured cancer treatment while raising her newborn. Then she went back to work at NOW Bank.

And today, she has some government wonk, high on the scent of his own gas, suggesting that her nearly 20-year career in cybersecurity is over? Caroline would use her significant influence to ensure that Prem takes Raykoff's job, and Raykoff gets demoted and shuttled into a less influential—and far less risky and damaging—position before she departs. It will be one of her final acts at NOW Bank.

Caroline is sad, but she isn't afraid.

8.

The Father

Another goddamn, motherfucking hassle, Victor Tanninberg thinks, as he contemplates the 1994 Corvette before him at Padraigh's place. He looks through his bag for some of his older equipment. *Another motherfucking hassle when I leave the house,* he thinks.

His phone is ringing. An ancient Samsung flip-phone he found on eBay because he despises Apple and Google. His son is calling.

He says he's going to a friend's house; he's hungry and is going to stop to eat along the way.

The voice Victor uses on the phone is a complete mismatch to the one in his head.

"OK, just be careful. Are you going to take the bus back from Steve's? All right. Want me to bring you home some Subway? Be careful, OK?"

Then he hangs up. Mutters a string of curse words under his breath. His son is good, shy, with a few friends he keeps close. He's quickly turning into an accomplished artist, and Victor has taught him to play guitar, one of his own hobbies.

He's also taught him to specialize in evasive maneuvers, not while driving but while living. Never attend large events in high-value-target locations like Madison Square Garden. Take the subway sparingly, and only to and from stations that are unlikely to be targeted by terrorists. Avoid Grand Central Station and Times Square.

Victor instructs him to avoid engaging in any political debate and recognizes that all teachers, especially those who teach in the public schools he attends, are probably intellectually limited.

Don't trust anyone who asks you for money or tells you a sad story about his life too soon after meeting him, Victor tells him. Never share any personal information until you've known someone for well over a year. If someone tells you they're not a good guy, believe them the first time. Never download any apps onto your phone. Never allow some company to track your location.

He worries he is too dark with the kid, but the kid smiles a lot. His boy humors him. Laughs sometimes at things Victor's not joking about.

Indeed, these are things a hacker actually worries about.

In fact, what worries him most is what he believes is an increasing lack of attention to detail in all things—engineering, security, car manufacturing. There's more stuff but so much of it sucks that it introduces more risk.

Victor immigrated to Israel from Russia when he was a child, and then to the United States when he was eight years old. His father, a government engineer, stayed behind in Russia while Victor, his mother, and Victor's older sister went ahead.

For several years, they lived without Dad, in a world of impossible freedom. It was the beginning of what would turn him deeply capitalist and conservative. He only works with American cars, he says frequently, because he loves America. From the get-go, Victor's father—who rejoined the family after five years in purgatory—

marveled at the inadequacy of American engineering and how it seemed to be growing worse as the years wore on. He referred to his own experience in industrial engineering—not computer code, but in bridges, tunnels, subway systems, and skyscrapers. He pointed out lopsided entryways and inelegant angles each time they would go into the city.

Victor sees parallels to this everywhere. Inefficiencies. Poor design. Lopsided and inelegant are the least of these. Sloppy code that invites problems. Sloppy thinking that invites manipulation.

It doesn't surprise him at all when computer engineers in Russia are able to do any number of things the media accuses them of doing. But he doesn't know that he would call it hacking. You can't break into a house whose doors have been left open.

You can't break code that was written with giant holes. You can't break weak minds. They're already broken.

9

The Teenager

René Kreutz never learned a single thing about evasive maneuvers from her father, even though he was a cop. He retired well before she was born. And he really retired. He sat down in a big, soft chair in front of a television and never—or so it seemed to René—got up again.

René's mother makes nice Romanian dinners and buys her good conservative clothes, but offers no life advice. When René asks either of them what they think she should do with her life, all they have to offer are blank stares. "Whatever you want, I guess."

René feels as if she is always tripping into and out of trouble, light-hearted trouble, but trouble nonetheless.

A few of the girls René grew up with and went to clubs with managed to wend their way into a life of casual prostitution. This isn't something René wants, so she leaves them behind. She gets involved romantically with a few feckless, aimless boys, but for no more than a few weeks. When they ask her for money, she rids herself of them quickly. She tries to be practical. Often in warm water but never hot.

Both she and Arnica Valka are growing up. And it's not just her nineteenth birthday that's making her feel wiser and older. It's much more concrete than that.

Arnica Valka is a quiet town, just 100,000 people, nestled in the foothills of the Transylvanian Alps, two hours west of Bucharest. It has, in fact, right under René's nose, become one of the world's most notorious cybercrime villages, with an underground economy funded almost entirely by ransomware, stolen credit cards, and identity theft. Media will later call some of its neighboring towns among the most "dangerous places on the internet" and "hackervilles." To her, it is just home.

René was born in Arnica and grew up in Nicolae Ceauşescu–era housing projects. About two years prior to her nineteenth birthday, she noticed her hometown changing. Tech start-ups were percolating in warehouses and old barns, furnished like American social media companies with beanbag chairs and exposed brick walls. René heard the pay at these start-ups was fantastic—too good to be true.

René never mastered math like her parents had wanted and had no desire to marry a nice, older rich man, as her mother had suggested. She decides to go into advertising. As a student in marketing at Arnica Community College, she fantasizes about landing a job in tech, but she can't write code. Besides, it's not like these start-ups she keeps hearing about actually advertise job openings. It is all very hush-hush.

In her free time, René likes dancing and reading detective novels. She smokes cigarettes with her friends that she rolls herself with fresh tobacco. She is paying her way through college by working at City Italia, one of the fancy new restaurants that has just cropped up to meet the demands of the tech economy. She jokes to patrons that her only tech skills are texting with one hand while pouring coffee with the other.

One thing René *is* good at is talking. She argues her way to better grades in school even when she has cut classes. She talked her way into a job at City Italia and talks her way out of parking tickets. She is pretty, too, slender with long auburn hair. Then again, most of the young women in Arnica are pretty. As the economy grows, she can't help but notice how the local pool of beautiful young women grows with it.

Sig Himelman first sees René at Sunday brunch at City Italia. He watches as she flirts with each table, just enough to get a good tip, but not enough give them the wrong idea. He sees potential in her right away. Sig sits with a group of other well-dressed, 30-something men. Tall and engaging, with a new, neatly trimmed beard and a brand-new set of custom-made white veneers, he's clearly the ringleader of the table. René flirts with him accordingly.

They talk in English—Sig with a German accent—but right away she thinks he asks too many questions for her comfort.

"How old are you?"

"Nineteen."

"Your voice is too low for a nineteen-year-old," he says.

"I roll my own cigarettes and I often forget the filters."

"It's a good voice. Reassuring. Do you like your job?"

René is always on guard for when a less-than-wholesome proposition might be coming. She leans in and whispers, "I am a child of God. You can find your whores elsewhere."

She grabs the tip from the table and walks away. He follows her and she debates whether to get the manager. No, she will handle this herself.

"Wait, wait," he says to her. "You misunderstood me."

She turns, arms crossed, and listens.

"I work at a company called TechSolu," Sig says. "We just opened a few months ago on General Maleur Street. We need a call center operator. Someone who sounds mature and who likes to solve problems. Whatever they pay you here, I'll triple it."

It sounds too good to be true, René thinks, but she wants a job at a start-up. Maybe this is how it works.

Sig can tell she's reluctant. He hands her his card along with a stack of crisp American bills.

"Meet me at the address on the card, Monday at nine a.m." He gestures behind him to the restaurant floor. "What do you have to lose?"

Monday morning, René finds herself walking down General Maleur Street, her father's pistol in her handbag, just in case.

The neighborhood is changed, indeed. Block by block as she nears the center of town, she sees new streetlights, more police cars. There are more people, too—young people—moving quickly in the cool morning air as they make their way to work.

Stores that once sold cheap cell phones are now vending expensive tablets. Computer servers are advertised in the windows like puppies. Some of the storefronts promote the fact that they accept Bitcoin as payment. René passes the old, yellow-drab laundry where her mother would take her when their washing machine wasn't working. It is now called Cafe Americain and looks just like a Starbucks.

Wedged between a health food store selling some kind of Korean drink with bubbles in it and a law office advertising financial crime defense is TechSolu. René grips her handbag a bit tighter as she enters.

Inside she finds a beautifully appointed open floor plan. The workers, all men, stare intently at their computer screens. Sig leaps up and greets her like an old friend, then ushers her into a glass office. On his desk, five laptops are stacked up like most people stack paperwork.

"I'm so glad you came, René!"

"I didn't think I would."

He offers her a seat and then leans back in his desk chair. "Do you know what we do here?"

"Technology, I presume," she says, raising an eyebrow. "But I am no good with computers. I am an excellent typist, though, and can certainly answer phones. I would require my first paycheck up front." She shifts her weight in the chair and smiles. Negotiating is a strong suit.

He smiles. "Do you speak any other languages besides English?"

"Russian and French."

"Both will definitely come in handy here. We have customers all over the globe."

René remains expressionless.

"We do penetration testing," Sig offers. "That is, we hack into companies and then they pay us to show them where they are vulnerable, so they can fix the problem. We're a cybersecurity company."

"Cybersecurity? Not hackers?" she ventures.

Sig grins. "Well, yes and no. We are hackers, but the good kind. Ethical hackers. White hats."

"So why do you need customer service?"

"Sometimes, when our clients have problems, they need to vent, they get mad because they don't like to find out that their computers were vulnerable. I'll be honest, sometimes they need to vent a lot. Or they can't figure out how to pay, so you have to guide them through the process. Most of our customers pay in Bitcoin, and it can be a little tricky for them to get it right."

"You don't pay your workers in Bitcoin, do you?"

"No. Of course not. You will be paid in leus or euros or U.S. dollars."

René knows of no legitimate business in Romania that gives its workers a choice to be paid in whatever foreign currency they want. But Sig is growing on her. He seems genuine and charming. And the workers in the open-plan office are all well dressed and appear happy. There are even beanbag chairs. It's just how she imagines working at Facebook must be, but on a smaller scale. Plus, she is really good at customer service.

"U.S. dollars," she says.

"Excellent! Let me show you your desk!"

Her desk is inside a small alcove office, slightly removed from the rest of the team so that she doesn't disturb them with her phone calls.

On her first day, René helps four "customers" transmit Bitcoin into a digital wallet held by TechSolu. The executives she speaks to on the phone are distraught. Sig explains the executives are angry because they don't find out how to fix the cybersecurity problems until after they pay.

She catches on quickly. The workers on the main floor of Tech-Solu are hackers and by no means ethical. They are breaking into American and European companies, freezing their important files, and demanding payment in exchange for a digital key that will unfreeze those files. Along with the digital key, TechSolu will also deliver a helpful PowerPoint deck on how to keep hackers like them from doing the same thing again. One of her colleagues sometimes gets on the phone, too, and walks the executives through what they did wrong.

Despite the consultancy feel, it's clear Sig and the rest of the team are cybercriminals. TechSolu's business model is ransomware.

But here they are, in a completely normal office, one that René really likes. They offer some health benefits. There is a football table. René rationalizes the criminal aspects away. *Cybercrime isn't the same as "regular" crime,* she thinks. *You have to be smart and savvy to pull it off. Plus, no one gets hurt, at least not physically.*

She sometimes gets a nice bonus in cash. Every so often, she tapes some of the cash in a small bundle underneath her desk in the office. Just in case.

What René lacks in computer skills she makes up for in street smarts. She quickly becomes hooked on customer service.

Every day, she talks to distressed businessmen and -women, calms them down, and explains that they have been hacked, that they can restore their data immediately for a small fee, and they can make sure it doesn't happen again.

The "customers" often go from pleading, crying, sometimes screaming to thanking her. Some even say that the money—often just a few hundred dollars—is a small price to pay for recovering their files and making sure it never happens again.

René soon learns that all tech start-ups on General Maleur specialize in ransomware or similar work. Above the Korean tea shop is a company that hacks into the databases of American retailers and steals credit card numbers. Next to Cafe Americain, another company buys those credit card numbers and manufactures fake credit cards that work like the real thing. They hire mules to go out and purchase goods that can easily be turned around and sold, thereby creating "clean" cash from the illegal credit card transactions.

Sig was wrong when he said he would triple her pay from City Italia. In fact, she makes four times what she had been making at the restaurant. She quits community college but uses what she'd learned in class to make TechSolu's PowerPoint decks prettier and more read-able. Soon René is optimizing TechSolu's ransomware racket.

She creates a much more compelling screen for customers to see when they are hacked. It no longer read "You've been hacked!" in green font on black. Now a subtler, almost reassuring message appears on an all-white background:

> We are sorry to disturb you, but a flaw in your operating system has
> allowed hackers to disrupt your operations. Your files have been
> frozen, but you have a number of ways to get them back.

She creates a menu of options for the customers, which allows TechSolu to increase its margins by 20 percent in only a few months. Most of the ransoms that clients pay are only around $300 or $400, but some are paying over $1,000 with the new menu. Clients can choose to pay quickly at a discount or wait and face an ever-increasing payment. If they do not pay by a certain time, their files will be de-stroyed. They can also pay extra for the latest and most up-to-date PowerPoint deck. In a few cases, René convinces customers to actually allow TechSolu's hackers access to their full network to do legitimate penetration testing. Sig promotes her, gives her a raise and her own glass office.

Shortly thereafter, one of TechSolu's hackers manages to get into a large technology company in San Francisco. A company René has heard of. The file cache the hacker accesses contains company emails, and a quick look reveals some very embarrassing messages from the CEO.

He is a well-known name, and as René pages through the trove, she is disgusted by his attempts to use vendor contacts to procure hookers. Other messages he sends internally to female employees include egregious innuendo and commentary on their looks and clothes.

René simmers. She's making good money, but this guy is a billionaire. Some executives at Sony had just been roasted all over the internet for far lesser crimes than these. *He needs to be put in his place,* she thinks. She churns through revenge scenarios in her mind, then hits on one that could be a huge win for TechSolu.

While the boys on the floor laugh about the treasure trove of filth they have hacked, René ducks into Sig's office.

"I have an idea. We contact the CEO and we ransom him for his emails. We don't ransom the company's files. We stay under the radar and spook him just enough to get him to pay up, but not enough for him to call the FBI. I'll reach out and explain the situation. I mean, how much do you think it's worth to him, a million dollars?"

"Do it," Sig says.

She researches the CEO but can't find a private email address, only a work address. She writes him something very discreet but references one email in particular, one that the CEO will know is from his emails: "I'll bet it tastes like chicken, but really good chicken." She shudders a little from writing it out, proofreads the rest, adds a burner phone number that will call back to her office phone. She uses the pseudonym Katrina and hits send.

It takes three minutes for her phone to ring, even though it is 1 a.m. in San Francisco. The call comes over a WhatsApp line—encrypted. On the other end, a tired man's voice with a surfer's affectation speaks.

"Hello? Is this Katrina?"

"Yes."

"I would like to ask . . . how much does it cost to use your . . . shredding services?"

"The current rate is two hundred Bitcoin."

"That's . . ." His voice trails off while he does the math, but she could have easily finished the sentence for him. "More than a million dollars."

"Yes," she says.

"And the documents . . . they are completely destroyed . . . after this service?"

"Yes."

She can, as she has grown accustomed to with other customers, hear him talk himself into accepting her proposal.

"Can you guarantee it?"

"Yes. I can put it in writing if you like and send it to—"

"No! No. That's fine. Your word is sufficient. After all, if you didn't keep your word, nobody would ever pay you again, would they?"

"No, sir."

Long pause.

"You have a nice voice. Where are you from, Russia? How much are they paying you? I'll bet you'd love to work in the U.S. H-1B visas are hard to get, but I just want you to know that I love women. I respect them."

"I'm sure you do, sir. If you don't pay within the next ten minutes, the rate goes up to three hundred Bitcoin. I will text you the details for sending the money to our wallet via WhatsApp. Have a wonderful evening!"

She hangs up, sweating. She turns around and can see all the hackers on the floor watching her through the glass walls of her office.

Her phone rings again. She ignores it. It rings again. She ignores it again. "Answer it!" someone yells. She ignores that, too.

Then a tiny ping from Sig's office next door. Only audible because of the dead silence. Then Sig's voice, ringing through the whole office, in German:

"Oh mein verdammter Gott."

Oh my fucking God.

He clears his throat, steps out of the office, and announces humbly: "Confirmed: 200 Bitcoin deposit."

$1.3 million.

Cheers. Whistles. René has pulled off the largest ransom in company history.

It is not yet 10 a.m. in Arnica Valka.

After taking a few moments to celebrate, René retreats to her office and sits down. A scene from her childhood plays on a loop in her mind.

Her father, a police officer, trying to teach her math at the kitchen table: "You must learn math and then computers. You can be an accountant, a nice office job." She put her forehead on the kitchen table over her folded arms, trying to ignore him.

Now she repeats the gesture on her office desk. What would her father, the police officer, think if he knew what she was doing?

Sig taps on the door and walks in. René looks up.

"How should we split it?" he asks. "You decide."

Typically, everyone in the office gets a piece of the ransom. It is a team effort, and if one goes down, they all go down.

"Evenly, just like all the others," she says. "It will keep them from fighting."

"Are you sure?"

"Yes. This isn't going to be the last one, is it?"

Sig smiles. All of their previous hacks had targeted companies and ransomed institutional data. This is the first time they have gone after a prominent individual. They hadn't so much deployed ransomware as they had committed blackmail, without the thinly veiled guise of offering cybersecurity services. TechSolu is about to pivot into a much more dangerous and much more lucrative business model.

That night, they go out to one of René's favorite clubs. She gets everyone cherry ChapStick-flavored cocktails. It's '80s night. René twirls with her colleagues to New Order's "Blue Monday," Depeche Mode, Prince. Sig sits in a corner, watching, sketching on his napkin.

He hadn't expected this. He likes it, that they have brought in so much money. But now there is René, the center of attention. A master criminal after just a few hours of work. With nothing more than a proficiency in PowerPoint and a God-given gift of talking to people she has all of TechSolu's employees spinning around her like satellites.

Sig realizes he no longer has control of the situation. He doesn't like this. He smiles at René, a big, sincere grin. She flashes one back, tipsy as she is, for a beat too long.

He's so handsome, she thinks, as a Guns N' Roses song comes on. "Welcome to the Jungle." *Such a good smile* he has.

Such nice teeth, she thinks.

Like a vampire.

10.

The Medium

Charlie Mack has been working nights and weekends to prepare for the public disclosure of what happened at NOW Bank.

When the company was breached and the rumors reached the media, it was a fucking free-for-all. People could talk and talk and talk about what they thought had gone down without knowing a thing. It was the not knowing that led to ridiculous, random speculation. That's why lawyers are so necessary—because disclosing the truth can dispel all their bullshit in one blow.

This propensity toward rumor-mongering was endemic to the field of security, including at Charlie's previous position at the CIA. Just before coming to NOW Bank, Charlie left his spy job, where he was stationed in Benghazi, Libya. He left right before the deadly attack on the compound there. Charlie Mack knows all about the dangers of speculation.

In NOW Bank's case, there are rumors that entire books of asset management clients have been snatched and that the hackers have control of high-speed trading platforms, that they could have taken down the bank or the whole financial sector itself. There are rumors that "they" are Chinese spies, sent in to monitor each and every activity of the bank. Or possibly Russians trying to get the financial information of either enemies or friends of Vladimir Putin. These rumors are mostly ludicrous but, like the best lies, contain a kernel of truth.

Some of the rumors, Charlie knows, have been spread around to various media contacts by Raykoff himself. In fact, there have been a few laudatory profiles in selected media outlets of the strong and tough military men the bank has hired.

But the positive coverage hasn't helped Raykoff. It became apparent to Charlie early in the investigation of the breach that Raykoff couldn't handle the pressure. He was replaced by Prem, first nominally, then literally, through an organizational shift.

Raykoff will eventually be moved into a more suitable job doing government relations work. Soon after that, he'll be reporting to Prem.

But for now, Charlie does what he does best. Saves the world, his world anyway, with intense attention to detail and an encyclopedic knowledge of cybersecurity law. The purpose of the disclosure is to spell out what happened as clearly as possible for the public while maintaining some degree of dignity for the bank. The disclosure will divulge most of the known knowns, a few known unknowns, and virtually no unknown unknowns.

Most of the latter two categories fall under law enforcement, and those enforcement professionals have the unenviable task of disclosing what must be disclosed to the public while leaving undisclosed the information that the Department of Justice wants to keep for itself to tout its own accomplishments.

Charlie takes a deep breath.

The "northern Italians" responsible for Venice are two Israelis and one Russian Israeli. They will be apprehended by the FBI and placed under arrest soon. There is a fourth guy, a mystery man named Tony Belvedere, who has been laundering money through Newark and Manhattan for the trio. This information will be kept under wraps. It is not for the bank to disclose.

The communications team is working alongside Charlie on a disclosure to media. To reaffirm the bank's commitment to cybersecurity, to maintaining the privacy and integrity of its customers' accounts.

It's Sunday and Charlie is wearing a pink button-down shirt, cargo shorts, and open-toed sandals. He's just returned from a short vacation to the Caribbean. He's trim and tan and looks more like a teenager coming back from spring break than a corporate lawyer. He talks in between document reviews to the other two workers who are there, Caroline and Frances, the communications lead.

Charlie is bored. He loved being a spy. In that job, he got to go to exotic places, do exciting things, know everything before it happened. Before it was disclosed. If it ever was disclosed. Benghazi. Malta. Morocco. Romania. He loves knowing secrets and, even more than that, keeping them. But he's a dad now with two young daughters. So no more spy stuff. This is as close to his old life as it gets for Charlie. The thrill of knowing a little inside info before it hits the press.

The fact is that all the rumors are vaguely true, they just aren't specific to Venice.

Did Chinese hackers get into the bank to steal all its secrets? Yes, but that was a while ago.

Are Russians trolling bank networks looking to grab information on Putin's "friends" and enemies? Sure. Just not in this particular case.

There are more important questions emerging from this particular breach. Are any of these things a matter of national security? Could the bank hold its own against fully funded international armies? Should it even be expected to?

The bank's relationship with its government "partners" is complex. For one thing, its government counterparts don't have the capabilities to truly help against these bigger, badder enemies, no matter what the various agencies claim. For that, they would need full visibility into bank networks. But the bank does business in many countries, not just this one. Giving the government that visibility would alienate a lot of important customers.

In addition, many government employees are champing at the bit to get the bank in trouble over other types of violations. It could get them a lot of street cred, a promotion, or, most important, a decent-paying job at one of the big consulting firms. Who knows, maybe some of them actually care about justice. So if the bank brings in a government agency every time there is a problem, the bank is going to get dinged by regulators, slammed by the media, and waste tons of time and money that could be better spent on actual security.

Everything is complicated. Nothing is straightforward. What Charlie knows best and what he puts more of his faith in than anything else is human intelligence.

The bank, the entire cybersecurity team—fuck, the entire cybersecurity profession—is relying too heavily on analyzing data. "Big data." Vast swaths of information streaming into little bank server bottlenecks, parsed by "artificial intelligence" engines, and interpreted into a spreadsheet or PowerPoint by kids two years out of college.

In Charlie's experience, this shit is useful for day-to-day problem-solving but meaningless in the long run. It "solves" nothing.

What *does* make a difference is the one guy or gal on the ground, in the trenches, doing the crimes or solving the crimes or watching the crimes who can illuminate the real problems and how they might be solved. Who are we dealing with? What motivates them? Everything else is just semantics. Charlie should know. He's the lawyer.

That's what he loves about Caroline. She knows the value of the human element. That's why she hired so many former spies.

The disclosure will go like this:

On August 5, 2014, we discovered a group of criminals had broken into our servers and stolen the personal details, including names, Social Security numbers, addresses and phone numbers of 87 million NOW Bank clients. We are working with law enforcement to investigate this matter and, as a result, cannot fully disclose some details of the investigation.

There is more to come. But this is good. Nice, straight, and to the point. Filled with crisp, safe known knowns.

Who was he kidding? People were going to freak out.

By Valentine's Day 2015 everyone in cybersecurity at NOW Bank is looking for a new job. If they haven't jumped already. Bonuses get paid out in a few weeks. After that, the real exodus will begin.

They were all promised sky-high salaries and big bonuses while they went slogging through the pain of Venice. Neither of which came to pass. Many people involved are of the opinion that this is due to Raykoff having pissed off so many people that they are putting the squeeze on him in order to further justify moving him out. Many of them, novices to the inner workings of the bank, have forgotten they work in a cost center. And once you find yourself in a cost center, you're always in a cost center.

Raykoff is busy today. He's meeting some important people. Some of the administrative workers in the SOC are surprised by a knock on the door. It's a man and a woman, both with earpieces, and another man behind them. They seem important.

"We're . . . looking for Bill Raykoff?" asks the one man without an earpiece.

The secretary answers. "Yes, he's upstairs. But I can let you in now."

The man is Admiral Michael Rogers, and the people with him are Secret Service agents. He's in civvies. Rogers is the head of the National Security Agency and Cyber Command, a centralized operations point for all branches of the Armed Forces and other agencies of the Department of Defense. He is there to see the SOC. He seems puzzled.

The secretary swipes him into the secure room. The door swings open. The SOC workers look up, slightly curious, then back down at their computers. Only one of them, a Navy vet, snaps to attention and salutes. Nobody else knows who Michael Rogers is.

Frances is now five months pregnant. She walks into the room and waves at Admiral Rogers and his entourage. "Howdy!" she says as she takes a seat.

Just a few moments before the admiral's arrival, she received an offer from a consulting firm that will more than double her salary—despite her being five months pregnant. She doesn't know who Admiral Rogers is and right now she couldn't care less. Between her house burning down and the breach, it's been a rough year.

But getting big offers and aggressive recruiter calls is happening to many of NOW Bank's security employees. Their phones have been ringing off the hook from recruiters.

There is now a premium price for the bank's cybersecurity employees. It's a seller's market for their skills. That's because they worked through Venice and thus have experience working on a complex, public breach, one of the biggest ever. Nobody hiring at other companies blames them for the breach. The top executives take the fall while the cybersecurity pros run.

Caroline will go to an insurance company, one populated by many of her best dragons who have already flown away. Charlie will stay, not for a lack of offers but because he keeps seeing daylight at NOW Bank as others peel off and everyone realizes he's one of a kind.

Prem will rise to the top. He's already replaced Raykoff and is sitting in his office. A new group will come in under him, and the ties that bind the old guard will wither away.

Raykoff is getting settled into his new role with a government relations theme. Things must be looking up because several employees visiting his new office have noted an industrial-size bottle of Viagra on his desk.

There are new criminals, too. Charlie is busy drafting an internal policy on how the bank and its executives will respond to ransomware and its rarer cousin cyber-extortion.

It's only a draft, though. Ransomers are targeting very discreetly now. He knows that will change once other criminal groups recognize the upside potential in the simple, cost-efficient attack. It's a new vector; he likes that. The concept, though, of compromising, extorting, and bolting is as old as spies.

He *loves* that.

11.

The Lovers

Sig smiles. He has regained control of the situation so he is smiling a *lot* these days.

René is at home, his home, the home he bought for them to live in together after a whirlwind romance. She doesn't come into the office anymore. It's better that way.

After her wild, overnight success, the guys at TechSolu started looking up to René in a way that threatened Sig's oversight of the enterprise. To combat this, he fell in love with her and ensured she did with him. Before she knew it, all her dreams for an exciting, high-profile, interesting life had been fulfilled. She was so star struck. Lovely, too. It was easy, and now she is still working for TechSolu but out of the picture. A perfect solution.

He has three business propositions he's considering. The first, something that will later be known as the post-Soviet bank heist, is just a fledgling scam right now. He has to go to Bucharest for the day to learn more about it. He doesn't like traveling these days. He's already put spyware on René's computer, though, and GPS on her phone, so he'll know what she's up to or if she leaves.

It is hard for René to believe that just six months ago, she was dancing in a club, celebrating her life as a newly minted millionaire. The phone contacts all over the world, the danger, the deception, demanding extortions from billion-dollar companies, it had been so sexy. That lasted about a week. But now she doesn't go to the club anymore. She doesn't even go to work. She got off social media entirely. Left her house and all of her friends. Her mother, who seemed to barely notice, has called her once.

Only six months, and now René works from home or, rather, an old farmhouse Sig bought for her and intends to renovate. It's big and airy and spacious, but she spends most of her time in it alone, in the smallest room in the house. She's even afraid to step outside some days.

In the beginning, it was amazing and romantic. Sig praised her endlessly: her ambition, her ability to think on her feet and make use of her meager education and average looks.

Meager. Average.

Then he encouraged her to cut ties with her college completely. Then, to work from his new home.

Or hers. He did say it is hers. That he'd bought it for her. But it is his.

Her friends couldn't believe it at first, that she'd settle down so quickly and so young, so he told her to stop talking to them. They are a bad influence, he says.

He says he wants to marry her, to settle in this spacious suburb in this big country house. But she feels her world has grown quite small. Where once she loved the freedom of being a waitress, and listening to music, and saying hello to her coworkers, and sharing her pictures with friends, all that has been replaced. First by work. Then by Sig. Thinking about him, worrying about whether he is happy with her, fearing she might do something to make him upset. Sig wants her to be better.

"Is there something wrong with that? I just want you to be the best."

So here she sits, working hard. He loves her. Right? That's what he says. He monitors her time online so it's difficult for her to leave. He texts her constantly, and if she doesn't answer right away, he gets worried. Or angry. Sometimes both. But she doesn't mind. He is just smitten with her. That's the word he uses. Smitten.

So she shrank down to the size of a pea. Even now, she's curled up in the loveseat, laptop in her lap, voice-over-IP to receive calls from ransom victims right in her chair. The calls come less frequently now. Companies have caught on. TechSolu gained a reputation as a crack operation that can be trusted to release data once it is paid. No need to call customer service.

René will miss the ransomware explosion that she in her own small way helped create. Her jaw tightens involuntarily. She wonders if she has a jaw problem. It aches and she doesn't know why. She feels something hot. Sig is always saying she seems too anxious. She can feel her jaw tightening, her teeth grinding. Is it nervousness, anxiety? Or maybe it's something else. What is the medical term for feeling trapped with no way out?

In Shanghai, Bo Chou is involved in a bit of a flirtation with one of his customers. The businessman is English but working in Senegal. He has a picture as part of his Fiverr profile—so few of them do. They take their conversation offline, flirting over Signal, an encrypted texting application.

But things quickly take a turn, when the client, who works for an oil company, starts asking him questions about where he gets his data. Bo goes with his usual lines, about public sources of information, SEC filings, and so on. But the client doesn't let up. "This info is too good, too personal, to come from public sources."

They'd been talking about far sexier things, and Bo's antenna goes up. He's only ever a few steps removed from his military training.

"I know for a fact that those email addresses you had for Saudi Aramco aren't public anywhere," the client writes.

Bo will drink himself into a stupor that night and go to work at the hotel the next morning hungover. But first he drops the phone on the bed like a hot potato. Then he deletes his chat history over Signal. Then he uninstalls the application. Then he wipes his phone entirely. Then, in a fit of pique, he drops it in the toilet and, after that, smashes it with a hammer.

Can't be too careful.

12.

The Researcher

It's nearing the end of spring in Romania, a beautiful June day. The Romanian word for spring is "arc." Sig likes that. His story and Tech-Solu's story are about to take another turn, so it seems appropriate.

Sig is looking over the shoulder of his cousin, a German computer expert named Dieter Reichlin, who looks much more the part of a hacker than Sig does, which amuses him. Dieter is tattooed from wrist to shoulder on both arms, with colorful scenes of outer space and fantasy planets that don't really exist. He wears a black T-shirt and black jeans and black leather boots, all cheap. His hair is long in the back and thinning a bit on top.

Sig has lured Dieter here so he can learn more about a scam that Dieter has written about but doesn't have the balls to pull off himself. That's the difference between the two: Sig is a man of action while Dieter sits on the sidelines and observes.

Dieter seems not to care about making money, which confounds Sig. *No matter*, Sig thinks. *More for me.*

————

Dieter is a security researcher. A legitimate one. He's visiting Romania. Doesn't love it. Doesn't trust it. Has to get a bunch of burner
phones to even enter the airspace.

Security researchers occupy an interesting subsegment in the cybersecurity field. They are typically independent engineers, hackers, or
intelligence gatherers. They offer freelance services and promote their
work through written articles or blog posts exposing various corporate
missteps or new types of cybercrimes.

They often get to know criminals or criminal organizations in
order to describe their crimes to the outside world. Dieter is a bit of
an anomaly. He is acutely interested in privacy research, and often
keeps his findings to himself.

Dieter believes Sig is under the impression that Dieter has no idea
that TechSolu is a front for criminal activity. This is fine with Dieter.
Sig has been vague about his reasons for moving to Arnica Valka. Sig
deflects any conversations related to his current work. Deflect, smile,
nod, move on. That's Sig, a master of deflection.

Dieter is a cousin related not by blood but by proximity. Their
mothers were childhood friends, so they had been forced together as
playmates and for family trips and had, by necessity, floated in the
same general direction their whole lives. Computer camps. Coding
classes, which Dieter excelled at and which Sig failed. Attempts at soccer, which Dieter failed and Sig managed better with his tall, lean
physique.

But for some reason, despite being taller and much better looking,
Sig never did as well with girls. That was always a sticking point, Dieter
knew, one he was wary of. Sig's flashes of anger could be cold and
scary, and he preferred to avoid them.

Sig and girls. Dieter had reminisced for the entire three-hour flight
here from Helsinki. Girls would flock to Sig in droves, attracted by

his good looks and charm, but only days or weeks later they would break up, the girls looking blank-faced and dejected, whispering to friends about Sig in a way that Dieter understood to mean that he was being blackballed in some fashion. And blackballed he was.

Growing up, Sig kept having to move in wider circles, outside their small town to neighboring villages, until those girls were whispering about him, too. Sig moved farther and farther away. Now he is all the way in Romania, and Dieter can't help but wonder what kind of girl he's got locked up in that new house he keeps bragging about.

To Dieter's surprise, when they became teenagers, it was he—short, a bit awkward but warm enough—who managed to do better with girls. For him, they were usually computer geeks, but he always had a pretty girlfriend who would stick around even after the breakup to be friends. Sig sneered at this, but he was clearly jealous. It drove the men apart. Dieter was not a psychologist, so he could not say why.

Dieter didn't like Sig, but he stayed close to him. This puzzling decision—puzzling even to Dieter himself—would only make sense later. Once Sig became a criminal and Dieter went on to be a researcher, he understood why. Because Sig made a very good specimen, and Dieter, an excellent scientist.

Three years prior to this flight from Helsinki to Bucharest, Dieter married a beautiful ghost-colored girl from Finland and settled there with the goal of having many pale children and quietly hacking computers for the purposes of good.

Around that same time, Sig got into some kind of trouble in Germany and ran off to Eastern Europe, and that's when the phone calls and visits stopped. Whether the trouble was with girls or computers, Dieter was never sure.

So then Sig was gone. Jet-setting, he said.

Dieter has ghostwritten a few articles in a German computer academic periodical about ransomware and criminal enterprises in Eastern Europe. He writes about social-engineering techniques in particular, the ones that involve people pretending to be someone they aren't by email, phone, text, even in-person meetings in order to get something from someone else fraudulently.

In one, where he was credited by name, he wrote about a particular ATM cash-out scheme that involved an especially tricky bit of social engineering—in this case, very slick fraud, the kind of work that suits narcissists and sociopaths. That's when he got an email from Sig, who was impressed with his research and wondered if he'd like to visit Romania. Bucharest is so nice this time of year, he wrote.

Dieter immediately agreed to the trip. Sig believed it was because his long-lost cousin must be bored with his married life and childcare responsibilities, because who would enjoy such things?

Dieter, always the researcher, merely wanted to know what Sig was up to, because Sig was a criminal. And Dieter tracks crimes and likes to write about them.

So around and around they went, making travel arrangements and small talk for a few weeks by phone and email, a light waltz of two oppositely charged magnets.

They settled on a good place to meet—a pub near the Bucharest airport. Dieter lies and says he can only spend the day before he has to return home. The plausible fiction: he must get back to watch the kids while his wife is on a business trip.

"That's terrible," Sig says.

"Yes, yes, what can I do? She wants to work, but you know women," Dieter had whined, his wife laughing silently and giving him the finger from the kitchen.

———

Now, here they are, in this pub in Bucharest. Sig watches expectantly as Dieter describes this new type of crime in detail. ATM cash-outs aren't particularly novel, but this particular approach takes it to a new level.

"It starts like this," Dieter says. "Let's say we are dealing with two locations. Bucharest in Romania and Tallinn in Estonia. You start with research. Banks have different kinds of ATMs, and some of them hold more money than others. Some hold up to $200,000. Most hold around $10,000.

"The $200,000 ATMs have a lot of things in common—they are older, connected with banks that don't have reasonable hours, and are often in areas where people do a lot of business in cash. These may be popular areas for mob activity or lots of Saudis or something like that. So you find out the First Local Bank of Tallinn has one of these big, overloaded ATMs. More research. When does the ATM get filled, what time of day? What car company brings the cash? When do they depart? Is the bank open or closed at the time? Does it see much traffic on that day?" Dieter pauses.

"You find the optimal location that meets all your criteria. OK, now you have your cash-out target."

Dieter has created a rudimentary PowerPoint presentation to illustrate this, on a crappy seven-year-old laptop. Sig frowns at it, pokes fun at how bad the PowerPoint is, comments that he knows somebody who could make it better. Dieter takes a drink of lager and ignores him.

"The next step is getting an account. Let's say you find a nice, small bank, the First Local Bank of Tallinn. It has a branch in Bucharest. So you get a mule, somebody you know well, who looks trustworthy. Like you! Not someone with lots of tattoos and bad clothes like me."

A sheepish smile from Dieter before he continues. "This good-looking mule opens an account at the First Local Bank of Tallinn in Bucharest and lists a Tallinn P.O. box as their address. They get a checking account with a debit card and a modest deposit and a credit card with a modest limit. The debit card and credit card for the bank are sent to the P.O. box in Tallinn, where you have another person you know, a money mule, pick it up. If you are—or a criminal is—working with a big network of people."

The next slide is taking a long time to load. Dieter feigns exasperation with the old laptop.

"You know," he says, "if you don't like the PowerPoint, I have a video presentation that illustrates this crime—it just won't play on my piece-of-shit computer."

Sig sighs, eyeing him cryptically. He reaches into his book bag and gets out a new, expensive laptop.

"Jesus, that thing is beautiful," says Dieter.

"You need to treat yourself," says Sig. "I'm sure budgets are limited with a wife and kids. But you need to have the best stuff if you are going to succeed in your business. I hope this woman knows that." Sig smiles pityingly.

"What can I do?" Dieter shrugs. "You know women." He tugs at the collar of his $2 T-shirt. His face turns red and his jaw tightens. He does his best to pass it off as shame, but something about Sig's casual cruelty sparks his anger, and he doesn't think it's their history together, not some sort of latent sibling rivalry.

At home, Dieter has a custom-built, state-of-the-art, completely segmented personal network. A fully automated smart home. He has three or four laptops far nicer than the beater he's using now. His yearly compensation is in the mid six figures, higher if he feels like pushing it. His wife is a successful accountant. Dieter doesn't need to brag about his wealth. Sig's weakness is his arrogance. Dieter knows this so he keeps his emotions in check.

Dieter gets a USB drive out of his pocket and sticks it into Sig's computer. Sig barely notices. Dieter continues praising the computer, its sleek lines and massive memory. He launches the video presentation about the ATM cash-out scheme from the memory stick. Unheard and unseen over Dieter's praise is the fact that a very specific, very insidious little piece of custom-made malware is already installing itself on Sig's computer.

The delicate little waltz between the two cousins continues. The video unfolds as a nice, clean, beautiful presentation, magically queued up right where Dieter had left off.

"So where was I? Oh yes, if you—or the person in question—is working with a criminal network, they will undoubtedly have mules already available in Tallinn for the next step. But if it is a smaller organization, usually someone very close to the criminal or the criminal himself will make the trip. The mule picks up the debit card from the P.O box in Tallinn and activates it, then waits."

"Waits? How frustrating!" Sig smiles, focused on the video, paying no mind to the USB stick. *Some criminal,* Dieter thinks.

"Now, the hacking part. Someone needs to install a back door on the bank's network, but discreetly. This can be accomplished with social engineering, convincing a system administrator at the bank to give up their login or password. Or phishing them. Or otherwise delivering malware that steals credentials. There are a few different ways of achieving it; it's a part of this particular scam that is not yet terribly well defined. However the method, you get into the bank's networks. You locate the account associated with the one that the mule just opened." Dieter pauses the video.

"The target here is the average daily limit for withdrawal and the credit limit of the credit card. You tick both of these up very high, to at least $200,000. Most accounts have a limit on how much you can take out of an ATM in one day, so you have to override that. And obviously, you need to have the highest possible credit limit."

Sig's eyes are wide as he focuses on the paused still of the video. Another round of lager arrives. "The bank doesn't catch the change?" Sig asks.

"They might; it depends. It depends a lot on their employees, who are watching for anomalies. But typically, no, at least not right away. That's why you do the next part very quickly. The mule in Tallinn takes the credit card, waits for the day the ATM is filled. He brings a burlap bag. Goes at night, with the appropriate clothes, a bit of a disguise. He puts the credit card in, types in some number, something just below $200,000, and the ATM spits it out. He covers the money dispenser with the bag and fills it up, then walks away. Some of them get away with a million in one day."

"What type of malware for the credentials?"

"There's one called August Malware that targets Microsoft Word documents, easy for most banks, though not Russian ones. There's Acecard and GMBot; both of those target the Android operating system." Dieter shrugs innocently, but he knows everybody uses Android in Romania and that Sig is paying close attention to this.

Sig is smiling softly now, getting a little drunker. He has it scoped out in his mind. He is getting tired of ransomware—too many other organizations are getting involved in it. This seems like a nice new step. And he already knows a pretty, auburn-haired Romanian girl who would make the perfect mule.

Dieter takes the USB stick out deftly and puts it back in his pocket. He feels more relaxed, too, partly because of the alcohol and partly because his malware trick worked. At the very least, it went unnoticed. And he will be on a plane back to Helsinki soon.

They talk about superficialities. Sig never mentions René. Dieter steers every sentence away from his wife and kids. They settle on politics. The upcoming election in France—Sig is sure the far right will win. In the American presidential election, a candidate named Donald Trump, a television star as far as Dieter understands, has just announced he will run.

"The whole thing will be a zoo, that is the only thing that I know," Dieter says. Sig drunkenly agrees.

"I don't think the woman who is going to run will be very popular," Sig says. "It will be interesting to see what the Russians do. They've been very active lately."

"Yes," Dieter agrees, this time truthfully. He checks his watch. Time to go.

13.

The Volunteers

By 2015, anyone who works in cybersecurity—criminal, good guy, or in between—can see that the Russians are more than active. They are so busy they can't train their hackers fast enough.

Cybercriminals are in high demand, especially by government-sponsored intelligence organizations. There are so many hackers in intelligence organizations and intelligence operatives involved in cybercrimes that even those in the know aren't sure exactly who they are dealing with.

This activity spikes during the lead-up to the 2016 U.S. presidential election, but the participants in Russia are so spread out, in terms of their geographic location, ideology, and backgrounds, that it doesn't appear like a coordinated effort. At least not to the untrained eye.

By this time, there is no longer a "farm team" from which to pull eager candidates into Russian cyberoperations. Recruitment has taken on a whole new angle.

The people doing bad deeds may have no desire to work for the government. They've never signed up for any patriotic mission beyond cheering on Russia in the World Cup. But they are being pressed into service by the government.

These young Russians are a lot like the young students at Caroline's hack-a-thon at NOW Bank. Instead of a conference room at the bank's headquarters, they are being recruited from all over Russia. A cup of tea and a recruitment pitch from one of Vladimir Putin's henchmen is more persuasive than Caroline's pep talk.

The recruitment process may be more modern, but one of their primary tasks is age-old. Election interference is an art, one perhaps first perfected by the British.

In 1940, British intelligence officers wanted to stack the American political deck with individuals who would favor U.S. entry into World War II. To do it, they tapped the phones of political candidates and used the deleterious statements they recorded in media campaigns against candidates who did not support their agenda.

They spread the news via a network of compromised journalists, who filed fake or exaggerated news stories to battle isolationist or neutral sentiments. In one case, they discovered that one of the political parties was taking donations from the Nazis. It's unclear how effective their efforts were, but it's likely the British had some influence on U.S. elections.

The truth is, every election, presidential or otherwise, is "interfered with" by some outside force. Every candidate has a series of nations behind him or her, loudly or quietly pushing for a win so that they can enjoy a relationship with the United States that furthers their goals.

There has been a series of changes in the past 20 years that has helped the Russians to be infinitely more capable than they were before. The first is a technically superior workforce of math wizards and computer hackers. What's more, now the government is willing to let those people—criminals, intelligence officers, or a combination of the two—work off the books with other nations in an effort to weaken U.S. infrastructure. Nations like Iran and North Korea.

And now they have ample testing grounds. The United States has sold or deployed its technology to many places across the globe. The United States is far less concerned about cyberattacks against infrastructure in Brazil or Ukraine or Mexico. But it's the same infrastructure.

The only way cybersecurity people get to be any good in this field is by doing the work. And for decades Russia has used the world as its lab.

Then there is the matter of shaky alliances. The ease of digital recruitment. Convincing government malcontents to give up their credentials is an art form that grows easier with the vast global exposure of the internet. But there's one thing that will never change and that, paradoxically, is the very human proclivity to change one's mind.

In Russia and other hotbeds of cybercrime, there is a long-established precedent that each individual employee, every government agent, each operative could wake up one morning with a sudden, irrevocable desire to pivot, to change directions, to switch sides.

René lies in bed, sick, feverish all over. She's pregnant. She's panicked, because she didn't think she could get pregnant. She worries Sig won't believe her. She checked the box of condoms he'd bought, which he says he has been using. But there is the box, unopened, shoved in a drawer in the bathroom, still in the bag.

Had he not been using them? She knows what he will say if she asks this question. He'll say she was delusional. Crazy. There was no way to bring it up without being accused of always accusing him of things.

"I treat you like a queen and this is what I get in return." His face will go from that pleasant mildness, that big, white smile, to teeth-baring rage in nothing flat. He will say she was seeing things, hearing things. "Maybe we need to get you to a psychologist?" he'll spit at her.

By June, she's figured out she is three months pregnant. She has been so busy, so distracted, that she hasn't noticed the missed periods. It is Sig who notices she is looking bigger around month two. He rids the house of carbohydrates. Insists she eat a diet of lentils and small portions of skinless chicken. She's hungry all the time, and now she knows why.

So she waits for him to come home. He said he was going to Bucharest to meet a business contact. Or was it an old friend? A cousin? She can't remember. It is all so mysterious; he is always so mysterious about where he is going and what he is doing.

He will be home late, past midnight. She hopes he isn't in the mood for sex when he gets home. She can't sleep because now that she knows she is pregnant, she can think of nothing else.

She fantasizes about going somewhere nicer than Romania, someplace really far away. In her wilder fantasies she escapes to England, America, the Caribbean. She imagines cashing it all in, her and Sig on a nice, warm island somewhere. Then maybe the old Sig would come back.

She is the girl who made those saucy phone calls to technology executives. Who shut down their advances with a crisp, cutting word or two. Tastes like chicken, ha, ha, ha. Now she is reduced to slicing and dicing her own internal monologue, for an audience of one. Well, technically, now two people. A baby. She can hardly believe it's real.

She stares at the ceiling, rubs her jaw. She has been reading a medical website's recommendations for jaw pain. She has ruled out many of the reasons for it—no tooth problems, no loose fillings or flu. The medical site has suggested a strange reason for it, one she hadn't expected: anger. Unresolved anger.

She ruminates on that point for a little bit. Anger, yes, anger. A strange feeling.

The Mother

14.

The Mother

The data isn't gone. It's just locked. Bo Chou is slightly panicked. He is the victim of ransomware, and his files are locked. Held captive. His beautiful data. He has half an hour to respond to the criminals who have attacked him. First the spy from Senegal, and now this. *Lie down with dogs, get fleas,* he thinks. It's too much.

The ransomware in question is called CryptoLocker, and he's done all the quick research he can on what it is, how to remediate it.

This isn't the same type of ransomware TechSolu uses, but an older, more rudimentary version. A more brutal type. Bo won't encounter any soft-spoken customer service representatives here. It's the automated call center version of TechSolu's full-service business.

Bo has gigabytes of research at stake. The criminals pitching him are Russian, it seems, or maybe even North Korean? It's difficult to tell through all the automation. They want $500, or the equivalent of that in Bitcoin. Bo is grateful that he has a little bit of cryptocurrency, enough to make the payment. He is ready to wire the money by smartphone, but pauses for a minute to contemplate what he's doing.

It's Halloween in Shanghai, 2015. The city has adopted the American holiday with a little too much enthusiasm, and people are screaming their heads off outside Bo's apartment window.

What Bo is experiencing is something on the brink of taking off, of turning into a global phenomenon. More sophisticated, smaller organizations like TechSolu have already pivoted to cyber-extortion: demanding bribes to bury damaging information, often for much higher figures. Automated ransomware is the latest trend because it can be spread virally and across many machines at once before being discovered. It's the Walmart of cyberattacks.

There's tons of ambiguity involved. It's rarely clear if the ransomers have access to the files they steal. Even some of the criminals don't always know what they have, but it's likely they are dealing with too many compromised files and machines to find out.

Bo is worried they have not only locked up his files but have downloaded them, as well. Losing the data would be devastating for his business. He kicks himself for not updating his damn laptop. He didn't want to take five minutes out of his day to do it, as if he didn't know better. It's unlikely that they have his data files, but he's not quite sure how CryptoLocker works, and even the information he can find about it on private forums is unclear.

Bo, stuck in his technological ways, never migrated his database to a cloud server—meaning all of the data exists on his laptop, stored locally. Years ago he had made a habit of backing up his data on a separate hard drive, but he grew lazy and stopped. This means all of his files are inaccessible unless he pays the ransom, gets the decryption key, and is able to open them back up.

Perhaps it is fortuitous, he thinks. He's been wanting to start fresh again. Maybe he shouldn't pay the ransom. Maybe he should leave those files locked up. Maybe he should stick to his hotel job. Maybe he should live a nice, clean life, find a nice girl or guy to settle down with.

Or he can pay the ransom, keep the data, and go completely in the opposite direction. There is an underground group he frequents on the dark web that's been discussing a lucrative scam involving just the kind of data he has been able to collect from his USB stick malware.

It works like this: Bo collects proprietary information strategically from selected, specific law firms, banks, or consulting firms. The information is about publicly traded companies and is nonpublic. In other words, information that could influence the company's stock price.

That information could include poor test results for a cancer drug if it's a pharmaceutical company or news that a big account had fallen through if it's a consulting firm. Other criminals in the group then put spyware designed to read keystrokes or observe the target through computer webcams to determine when the news is going to be released.

Then the group buys and sells stocks in anticipation of the news. And they almost always win. They are raking in millions in the stock market, way more than the pocket change Bo was making on Fiverr.

Then there's the craziest option of them all: Bo leaves the life of crime and gets a legitimate job. He has received some interest from an American company with offices in Singapore. The role would be in big data and analytics. The offer had come from one of his Fiverr clients, a frequent flier. The guy is an executive who runs a small business unit covering southern Asia. He is impressed with Bo's ability to gather such intricate knowledge about certain companies. The executive has no reason to disbelieve Bo's story, that the information is all gleaned legitimately.

Bo could get a visa to Singapore, a luxurious and exciting nation, even more exciting, perhaps, than Shanghai. But he'd have to give up his data collection activities and change his lifestyle entirely. An American company wouldn't tolerate his data harvesting, and he couldn't risk getting on the wrong side of Singapore's legal system. He'd probably have to live in fear of all the risky stuff he'd done.

He stares at the computer screen. It looks like this:

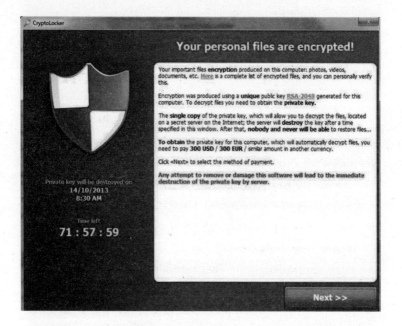

Outside, the crowd is getting louder. Drums and music have started up. He realizes 10 more minutes have gone by. He now has only a little over an hour to decide, before all his data is destroyed. He notices a voicemail on his phone. Doesn't recognize the number.

He puts the phone on speaker and nearly falls out of his chair. It's his mother. He doesn't even know how she got this phone number. It's been nearly a year since he's heard her voice. She is firm, as always, but there's a bit more emotion there. Dad has been sick with the flu, she says. They're so grateful for the money that he sent them six months ago. She misses him.

Bo's mother is from Kashgar in the far west of China, close to Nepal. She is a Buddhist. She clings to tradition. She tried to shape him into someone just like her—hardworking and satisfied with a dull but safe life—but she did not succeed.

Kashgar was once a critical trading post on the Silk Road. Bo enjoys reading about its history. It was one of the things that attracted him to the dark web, when an illicit marketplace by the same name rose to prominence there.

The Silk Road was an integral route for trading between China, Korea, Japan, India, Iran, Europe, the Arab world, and the African continent.

It wasn't only silk that was traded. Islamic and Christian teachings made their way across various parts of the world through this route. Art, literature, and philosophy spread, as well, alongside cultural traditions, languages, and cuisine.

When Bo was young, his mother would tell him tall tales about the original Silk Road. It was a rare show of warmth on her part and one of his better childhood memories. One of his favorite tales was about the tradition of sand mandalas: elaborate, colorful sand sculptures made by Buddhist monks that, once completed, were destroyed in a religious ceremony.

She would tell him of the shocked looks on the faces of Arabs and Jews and Europeans after witnessing this sight on their travels through Kashgar. She acted as if she had been there. He would laugh at the foreigners' surprise as the monks blew the sand away. All that work, all those beautiful designs—gone.

This is the high school textbook version, of course. Kashgar's ancient trading post saw far darker exchanges than feel-good stories like the ones his mother used to tell him. Slaves were brought thousands of miles and traded along the route. Concubines captured by Vikings were sold in Dublin and young men captured by the Turks were sold to fight wars across the Ottoman Empire. The Silk Road was a prime route for carrying viruses and bacteria—including *Yersinia pestis*, the Black Death.

The dark web Silk Road was, by contrast, mostly remembered for its pestilence. Founded in 2011, it served as a vending point for drugs and firearms. It also was ground zero for a certain brand of libertarian idealism characteristic of its founder, an American computer programmer named Ross Ulbricht.

Ulbricht, who is currently serving two life sentences for drug trafficking and other crimes that were perpetrated on the digital Silk Road, created the space as a kind of freethinking exercise.

The Silk Road was accessed, like most dark websites, by using a virtual private network and downloading a specific browser. Designing the browser took computer programming skills that Bo admired but did not himself possess. Learning about the massive global marketplace for cybercrime and falling in love with it, however, was just as addicting as Facebook.

Sixty minutes have passed.

Sand mandalas. The impermanence of love and hate. The way the past reaches into the future. Bo's imagination has roamed the space between here and there, good and bad, white and black.

Now he has 10 minutes before the ransomware eats his past five years of hard labor. He opens the email from the American company's Singapore office and reads it again. It's not a hard offer. It's not a certainty. Three minutes. He reviews the chat history with the insider traders who want him to join.

One minute.

He closes his laptop. Throws it into a plastic bag. Ties it up. Smashes the bag with a hammer. He throws it in the garbage, presenting his data to the wind like a monk's sacrifice.

He composes a note to the executive in Singapore expressing his great interest in the opportunity. Next, he does something that he hadn't even contemplated 72 minutes ago.

Bo Chou calls his mother.

15.

The Ghost

Victor Tanninberg is having lunch with his journalist friend. It is early November 2015, and he hasn't been outside his house in what seems like a year.

She has hundreds of questions for him. Especially about the upcoming election. She's been getting lots of weird chatter about hacker activity during the 2015 primaries. And she wants to hear about the cars he's been working on, about hacking in general.

"I'm not a hacker," he insists, over and over again. "Yes, I have a Russian background, but I don't know what the Russians are up to—that's ridiculous."

They have burgers at a pub. They drink beer. He shows off pictures of his kid.

In the end, he admits, leaving his house wasn't too terrible. He has had what most people call "fun." He might even do it again sometime.

It's a quiet day in Helsinki. Dieter Reichlin has finished reading *The Girl with the Dragon Tattoo* for the second time. The book, which is ostensibly about a slim, angry hacker named Lisbeth Salander, makes frequent references to the various types of sandwiches—tomato and mozzarella, egg salad—eaten in Scandinavia.

The first time he read it, he was left with an unstoppable hunger for egg salad sandwiches. In anticipation of his finishing the book a second time, Dieter's wife has mixed up a big bowl of egg salad. He sits, now, in his underwear at the breakfast table, eating egg salad right out of the bowl and watching Sig Himelman try to pick up women on Craigslist 1,700 miles away.

It is not what he'd expected. TechSolu or whatever Sig calls that place was a tiny criminal speck, but one that appeared to have been operating efficiently.

Dieter is interested in seeing if Sig will try the ATM cash-out scheme. At first, Dieter was sure he would, but Sig's crack operation seems to be fraying at the edges. After watching the litany of flattering, saccharine messages to girls across Romania, he wonders if Sig even has time to work at all.

One event flagged his attention. Directly after their meeting in the Helsinki airport, Sig opened a new bank account at Arnica Valka's branch of Banca Transilvania on his laptop.

He did it using the identity of a young woman. It appeared to be a stolen identity, someone named René Kreutz, with an address in a suburb of the city.

It was the only inkling that Sig would branch out into this new scam, and then it was gone. Otherwise, besides the Craigslist solicitations, Sig remains balls deep in cyber-extortion. It isn't clear who the victims are, but the payments—usually in the five- to six-figure range—keep rolling in.

It caused Dieter to rethink how he viewed his former rival.

Dieter had long viewed their relationship as a meeting of equals and opposites. Black and white. Good, simple Dieter and bad, complicated Sig.

This was changing things. Reading Sig's messages, the flowery language, the grasping at straws with women he doesn't know, dispels the illusion of a cool and confident criminal mastermind.

He had imagined Sig as a powerful executive with an army of underlings, or "employees," as Sig would call them. In this reckoning, Dieter had pictured someone who comes across as a legitimate boss, making his charges feel better about the bad things they are doing, the risks they are taking. Through the handful of exchanges he can see on Sig's laptop, however, he detects someone who is not in complete control, a personality that is deteriorating.

Dieter had fantasized about the incredible white paper he could write about Sig. Tracking the criminal element, offering a detailed look at how a cybercriminal operates, getting inside his head.

Now he isn't so sure. As with many types of spyware, Dieter's visibility is myopic. He can see only one piece of the puzzle, and it's getting him nowhere.

He has some view into Sig's transactions and his keystrokes, but it is difficult to connect the dots. Dieter hates spyware. Even the type that can co-opt webcams offer limited visibility. You can only see a single subject—if it's a camera on somebody's computer—or a stationary space, watching people walk in and out of a building. Unlike Lisbeth Salander, who could in her fictional world seemingly monitor everything about everyone simultaneously from an old Nokia smartphone. He laughs to himself, then frowns.

Because despite the obvious downside, here he is, still watching Sig. *Perhaps,* he thinks, *this is more personal than practical.* He shuts his laptop and digs into the bowl of egg salad with a large soup spoon. He will check back in a week to see if Sig has tried to open the bank account.

There's a sudden commotion on the stairs leading to the kitchen. It's his wife, the kids. Two daughters, from deep asleep to wide awake in a second. Insane, ghostly children. Hair perpetually a mess. His wife is pregnant again. She glares at him.

"You have egg hanging out the corner of your mouth."

"It's that damn book."

"Watch your language."

The children shriek: "Damn! Damn! Damn!"

"I'm sorry."

"You will want tomato sandwiches next."

"I can get some at the store. Later. Tomorrow. Next week." *Whenever suits you, my love.*

He smiles. She smiles back.

She picks up a month-old newspaper from the rack. Reclines on the couch. He reads the unspoken signal.

It's your turn to mind the children.

He drops down to the floor on his hands and knees. "Who wants to ride the horsey?"

The children cry: "Me! Me! Me! Damn! Damn! Damn!"

René Kreutz is exhausted. Eight-months-pregnant exhausted. She reclines on her side on the couch while Sig clicks away at his laptop at the kitchen table.

He's been bothering her for days to go downtown and set up her own bank account. She has no idea why. *It's utterly ridiculous,* she thinks. He insists it's for the baby. His arguments make no sense, and she's too tired to do anything about it other than politely decline.

She doesn't want to go into town and risk running into someone she knows. She's embarrassed about being pregnant. She's perpetually embarrassed these days. The girl who never got herself into hot water is boiling.

She drifts off into a sort of half sleep. In her daydream, she goes through the motions of what a best-case-scenario childbirth will be like. The epidural. Sig by her side, offering support. Nice nurses dressed in white. She's in the bedroom, the same one where she was born. Her mother will come later, after the birth.

"Could you stop breathing so loudly?" he says, startling her slightly. She complies, staring at the wall in misery. She's frowning without realizing it, something Sig forbids in the house. He looks up. "What did I tell you about frowning at me? Why don't you smile sometimes? You need to smile more. You look old like that."

She smiles at him, but he's staring at her. He looks afraid, an unusual expression for him.

"Yes?"

"Look at your legs."

René looks down.

Blood everywhere. She hates blood.

René turns white as a cloud and passes out.

16.

The Recruiters

The market for cybersecurity jobs is hot and it's not likely to change anytime soon. There are so many open jobs and so few people who can do them that many firms predict millions of open jobs over the next 10 years. Far more of those jobs will go unfilled globally, where skills are in even shorter supply than they are in the United States.

Cybersecurity education is deficient. It's hard, if not impossible, for people to get experience in the field, and many of these jobs require experience.

The following are generalizations, but legitimate ones: People with strong technical backgrounds frequently have a hard time making it in the corporate world. They may, like Victor Tanninberg, be excellent programmers and exceptional mathematicians, but they have little taste for politics, paperwork, or being required to show up between the hours of nine and five. Some people hate wearing a suit; others can't follow rules.

People with a corporate background often can't get the experience necessary to transition to security. They may be excellent at managing projects or leading a team of people, but the rote requirements for cybersecurity jobs—various certifications, for instance—keep them out of those roles. An investment of six weeks can turn a generalist into a good cybersecurity professional. Somebody talented, like Charlie Mack, for instance, can come from an intelligence and security background with a law degree and can learn the cybersecurity side in an instant. Most companies aren't willing to take that kind of gamble.

People in the military have a full range of security skills, but they get little help going from the highly structured environment of the government to the free-for-all that is the private sector. Some big corporations, like NOW Bank, tackle this by giving veterans mentors who can help them understand the protocols of the enterprise. Chief among these lessons is that crossing hierarchal lines is more acceptable, and sometimes even preferred, in a corporation than it is in the military.

This type of mentorship has helped countless veterans make a smooth transition to lucrative cybersecurity careers, like the employees Caroline Chan plucked out of obscurity to work at NOW Bank. However, military brass like Bob Raykoff, who have been in leadership positions for a substantial amount of time, don't always think they need this type of training, and before they know it, they inadvertently alienate huge segments of their organizations.

There is, as Victor points out, a significant lack of experts who are both proficient and savvy enough to do truly original cybersecurity work. The very good ones are quickly courted by the largest technology companies, followed by the banks and start-ups, with other types of companies, like healthcare firms and hedge funds, bringing up the rear. Those who are left often go to the government. There are many government cybersecurity employees who are highly proficient and true believers in their mission, but no one is under the illusion that a good hacker will be satisfied with making $50,000 a year for the National Security Agency when he could be pulling in four times that much at Google.

There is also a lack of people with truly good social-engineering skills. When a malicious person calls you and convinces you they are a help desk employee and you need to give up your username and password to prevent a problem, that's social engineering. When he says he's a Nigerian prince and needs your help, that's social engineering. When they open an account under a fraudulent name and identity at a bank branch, they are socially engineering the bank branch manager with a wink and a smile.

This is social engineering, taken from the 2018 indictment of 12 Russian hackers accused of infiltrating the Democratic National Committee:

On or about June 8, 2016, and at approximately the same time that the dcleaks.com website was launched, the Conspirators created a DCLeaks Facebook page using a preexisting social media account under the fictitious name "Alice Donovan." In addition to the DCLeaks Facebook page, the Conspirators used other social media accounts in the names of fictitious U.S. persons such as "Jason Scott" and "Richard Gingrey" to promote the DCLeaks website. The Conspirators accessed these accounts from computers managed by POTEMKIN and his co-conspirators. On or about June 8, 2016, the Conspirators created the Twitter account @dcleaks_. The Conspirators operated the @dcleaks_ Twitter account from the same computer used for other efforts to interfere with the 2016 U.S. presidential election. For example, the Conspirators used the same computer to operate the Twitter account @BaltimoreIsWhr, through which they encouraged U.S. audiences to "[j]oin our flash mob" opposing Clinton and to post images with the hashtag #Blacks-AgainstHillary.

People who can do this type of work are incredibly hard to find, because they often don't realize they can do this type of work. Having a technology degree doesn't help, but being a social butterfly certainly does.

This is why Russian intelligence operatives have thrown in with criminals, because they are good at these things. They aren't wonks. They find your soft spots. This is why Bo Chou, when he decides to go legit, will be so good at his job in Singapore—because unlike many other strong technicians, he knows that running down a taxicab and rescuing a customer's passport is a key to success despite the fact that there is no immediate payoff for him.

It is also why, when René wakes up in the hospital, she will be eminently employable. Even if, in a fog of shame, she doesn't realize it yet.

"Placenta previa," says René. Her mother cuddles the baby, a boy, not yet named. "That's what they called it."

It was the lining of her uterus. Stuck in the wrong place. It caused some bleeding and she had to have an emergency C-section. Baby is fine. Mama is fine. She is in pain, but opioids are making everything better.

Sig paces nervously. He's been spending the past hour alternately charming René's mother and the nurses, talking about how worried he was for René and the baby. His baby. He seems thrilled, but René has grown wise in the past 24 hours.

"I'm so exhausted," Sig says.

René's mother tries to hand him the baby, but he demurs. Looks at his mobile phone. Picks at his cuticles.

René's mother pats him on the back, asks him if he'd like to go out for cookies. He says yes. René is grateful her mother is there to help, and to keep Sig out of her way.

17.

The Insider Threat

By April 2016, ransomware has become so prevalent that many of the criminal organizations that pioneered it are breaking apart at the seams.

But Bo Chou couldn't be happier. The financial firm in Singapore offered him a contract. He was worried it wouldn't work out. But the boom in this new kind of criminal enterprise means his inbox is overflowing with interesting work. Work he is very good at.

Bo is in the midst of helping write a ransomware policy for his company and translating it into several languages. Just the other day, he helped coach a department through a difficult ransomware attack. They were able to avoid paying the ransom after verifying that all of the locked data was held on a cloud server. Now he's writing a proposal to move all data backups to cloud servers in advance of what will become a much larger and more damaging wave of ransomware. His boss is thrilled. They might even win a bigger budget.

From a drab cubicle on a red dot in the middle of Asia, in a glamorous high-rise office far removed from his drab military days, Bo silently high-fives himself.

Absolutely no one at TechSolu is happy. All the workers are getting recruited by other criminal groups. Some of them, Sig knows, are plotting to go off on their own as independents. Some of them, Sig suspects, are planning on stealing his intellectual property before they do.

Sig tries finding a new woman for the office, but it hasn't yet worked out. The guys want René back, but he told them she didn't want to see them anymore. That she's too busy with the baby. They are offended. Sig shrugs. *You know, women . . .*

Based on his recent searches, Dieter knows that Sig is worried about insiders at his enterprise making off with his criminal trade secrets.

Dieter has been leaving Sig's feed alone in recent weeks. He's been thinking about a number of projects and thought pieces on ransomware. As a researcher, he is somewhat lazy and easily distracted, but he's curious about one of his favorite topics: insider threats.

What Dieter loves most is the inevitable and ultimate failure of organizations attempting to find someone who is threatening their business from the inside. It's like trying to rid a house of mice. You think they're there. You imagine you hear them scurrying. Sometimes you catch a glimpse of a darting gray form across the floor.

But human beings are even less predictable than mice. They easily have a change of heart. They are able to evaluate their priorities and change them on a whim, reconsider their decisions, and turn into completely different people.

Edward Snowden, for example, was a good and trustworthy Booz Allen Hamilton employee before he turned into the infamous figure we know today. The only difference was a change of heart, a shift in thinking, from doing an engineering job he enjoyed to being offended by government oversteps to going rogue.

Chelsea, née Bradley, Manning was an Army employee with a history of filing complaints and small behavioral problems, but not enough to put him on the front burner for discipline, when she was charmed by the online community at WikiLeaks. So convinced was she by these latent online friendships that she went from being a middling employee to committing high espionage.

History is filled with examples of decent, hardworking people who, upon experiencing a startling revelation, suddenly and irreversibly become insider threats.

And here is Sig with his tiny criminal enterprise, Googling "how to find an insider threat." *Good luck with that,* Dieter thinks. His employees wouldn't need much of a reason to turn on Sig. His compatriots are criminals, after all.

René doesn't care about TechSolu's troubles, or being ostracized from the workplace, or the fact that she's so young and is now a mother. She has a little baby boy named Henry. He's lovely. She's breastfeeding him.

Henry. She calms at the sound of it. It's not a name so much as a course forward.

Sig has noticed her sudden shift in loyalty. It's made him even less pleasant but also kept him away more often. He's never home, and when he is, he's a terror. Everything is a reason for a fight. He yells at her in the morning, at dinner, in front of the baby, while she's breastfeeding. The harder she clutches Henry, the louder he yells. The louder he yells, the closer she pulls the baby to her. It's a ridiculous spiral that must end soon.

She hasn't seen other people for ages. But that is going to change.

Despite Sig's efforts to keep René away from the TechSolu office, he still wants her to come down to show off the baby. They plan on going today.

Henry is so cute and perfect looking, after all. Shiny dark hair and light eyes. "He looks just like me, don't you think?" Sig says as they head outside to his BMW. René stares straight ahead, her pretty mouth flat as a dash on her face.

"I'm sorry," she says in a monotone.

Sig smiles.

At the office, René thinks things look different. They smell different. Several seats are empty. The remaining guys glare at her, follow her every move. She senses their suspicion but doesn't understand its origin. She doesn't really care. She can withstand their looks. She won't engage in their workplace drama. She has nothing to explain to them.

Sig gives her some money for lunch, fans the bills out in front of everyone so they can see how generous he is. Sig says he has to get back to work, that she should go down to Café Americain and grab whatever she wants. He keeps his arm around her as if he's reluctant to let her go and wears a huge, unflinching smile.

"Everyone here misses you!" he says.

She smiles halfheartedly.

"You're so shy these days," he says.

She nods again. Doesn't speak. Doesn't make eye contact. She takes baby Henry out of the carrier around her chest, briefly shows him off like Simba in *The Lion King*. He wakes up, fusses. "He needs to feed," she whispers to Sig. He directs her to the ladies' room. "What about my old office? It's more sanitary," she suggests. He ushers her in, lets her sit. Closes the door. Gives her five blessed minutes of privacy.

She puts Henry on her breast, then reaches under the desk, her fingers feeling around the fiberboard underneath. There it is. Taped just where she remembers it. $1,000 in cash. She stuffs the money into her bra.

It is a gift, she thinks, left to her by the old René, the one who packed a pistol in her purse on her first trip to TechSolu.

18.

The Terrorist

The new dark web Silk Road is where Brendan "Tahir" Gerie likes to spend most of his time these days, and in spite of himself, he keeps getting tempted by the less refined wares the service has to offer, like this one:

FRESH, NEW UPSKIRTS. HOT YOUNG TIGHT UNIQUE. FREE WITH YOUR PURCHASE OF THESE AMERICAN RETAIL CC NUMBERS.

He hovers his mouse over the chyron. He could use some more credit card numbers. The price is reasonable. And, of course, the value proposition is high.

But is it halal? Probably not. Depends on the girls, though. Maybe they are Muslim, and if it was unwitting, or if they were tricked, then it is not their fault. So maybe he can look? He's confused, consults an ISIS messaging board that he frequents. He waits for several minutes. No answer to this pressing problem.

He prays, has to start over again four or five times. It's March and it's hot in Singapore. *HOT HOT HOT.*

Brendan goes back to his previous assignment. Finding identities on the dark web that could be of use to ISIS.

He posts again, this time on a chat board with other terrorists. He buys credit cards elsewhere. He trades for them using a rootkit that he has customized slightly and loaded onto a variety of popular pornography websites. Anyone who visits them will have malware downloaded onto their computers, a botnet for minor-type cyber-attacks like DDoS. He doesn't care. These people deserve it. It is his right to ruin their computers, because he is pure.

These things are bad, corrupting to the human mind. That's why he designed it. Rootkits are important tools, made of software but no different from the shovels and spades ISIS is using to create a new and better civilization in Syria. He will fight for his brothers using his engineering degree and his heart, which is *just like a lion's heart.* Fucking women. None of them ever appreciate this about him.

Brendan is from a suburb of Galway, Ireland, called Ballybane. A drab and gray place where he grew up in ivory-white public housing. He traveled the world and managed to get a few engineering certifi-cations and make a decent living along the way, but he never made enough money to entice a woman to pay him any mind.

He likes Singapore. It's clean and quiet, and he can go about his business undisturbed. He uses a virtual private network to access the dark web because, despite its many advantages, Singapore is still run by *the thought police.* To anyone trying to spy on him, it looks like he's doing straight work, coding and fixing bugs for merchant websites on a freelance site called Fiverr. He does this on his "straight" laptop, which he connects to the local network. On a different laptop, how-ever, the signal is routed through a server far away in Kiev using a virtual private network. Anyone trying to locate him will think he's operating from Ukraine.

Local law enforcement agencies know all about him, but he's not really doing any damage. The information he's trading is irrelevant. But they're watching. They know how VPNs work, too.

Dieter Reichlin is also watching. He likes to read Tahir's ludicrous posts, especially now that he is writing about cyberterrorism.

There are two types of cyberterrorism, and Dieter is trying to distinguish between them for a possible article, which he is not sure he'll ever be able to finish. He wants to find the parallels between the two.

There is the type of terrorism that everyone fears: the big, sweeping attack that takes down an entire country's electrical grid or causes a nuclear facility to overheat.

But there is also the more personal type, the kind Tahir perpetrates, attempting to take low-level, rudimentary hacking tools and turn them into something that can be used to move his own personal agenda forward. This philosophy is behind many different types of attacks, of course, but Dieter wants to understand the agenda so he can make sense of the action.

Bo Chou is also watching people like Tahir. He's permitted to go on the dark web as part of his job. As ISIS has proliferated, so have the armchair warriors who want to support the terrorist network. A fascinating bunch, and a legitimate reason for him to visit the very latest incarnation of the Silk Road.

Despite the large numbers of people like Tahir on the internet, there has been only one successful prosecution of a cyberterrorism case in the United States.

Ardit Ferizi was a Kosovar Muslim living in Malaysia who used stolen credentials from military bases to supply a kill list to ISIS. In order to do this, Ferizi used a rudimentary attack technique called a SQL (pronounced like *sequel*) injection—abbreviated as SQLi—in which malicious code is injected into a database in order to corrupt it and, in this case, extract information. Ferizi targeted retailers on military bases not only to steal names and addresses of government personnel who may be living overseas, in reach of actual ISIS fighters, but to provide those names to high-level members of the terrorist group.

Here's a real interaction between Ferizi and Junaid Hussain, an ISIS recruiter, captured by the Department of Justice:

> **Ferizi:** Elhamdulilah brother :)
> wait i prepare some dumps i got ok
> **Hussain:** which website akhi
> **Ferizi:** [Company Name Withheld] :)
> Plus i got
> the credit card
> of airforce
> department
> waiti show u
> [Company Name Withheld] have around 190k users
> :)
> orders.html
> **Hussain:** Where u get the mil/gov dumps?
> **Ferizi:** in the website [Company Name Withheld] already now I'm connected on it
>
> —
>
> **Ferizi:** I have also another shop which have 878k clients and its a military shop
> :)
> there is huge db [database]

—

Hussain: how did u get DB access?

Ferizi: easy penetration

Hussain: SQLi?

Ferizi: sqli the mobile app :P

And got access all in

Hussain: masha'Allah

Hussain: nice

Ferizi: everyday 400/500 orders come in this website [Company Name Withheld] :)

Hussain: But how you got DB login info

Ferizi: penetration after penetration

Injection after injection

Ferizi, who was 19 years old when he committed these crimes, would later be extradited to the United States, tried, convicted, and sentenced to 20 years.

Bo Chou has been eagerly following Ferizi's story. He has settled into a modest apartment provided by his new employer. His managers overlooked a number of holes in his resume to give him a job monitoring for insider threats, because they couldn't find anyone else with the skills to do the job. They have sophisticated software tools that help him visualize the activity of all of the company's employees.

He is like an ex-smoker who frequently seeks out information confirming the wisdom of his decision. And Ferizi's case is just another one of those reference points, an example of what can happen to you when you go bad, when you pick up that cigarette again.

He knows it's not the same, though. There are always a few smokers who live to be a hundred. And this sometimes keeps him up at night.

When he thinks about what could have been, he often goes back to one of his former associates: Nat Oren, an Israeli hacker who seemed to embody this moral ambiguity so perfectly.

Israel itself seemed to be churning out Nat Orens, in fact. It's easy to become a cybersecurity expert in Israel, as easy as getting a degree in English in England or business management in New York or comparative studies in Portland, Oregon.

Cybersecurity education starts in earnest in middle school there, and in many cases, even earlier. The population is small, agile, security-minded, and entrepreneurial. Nearly everyone gets military training. And in many ways, they dominate cyberspace. Proof, on a larger scale, that tight, small, and smart in the world of hackers may win out over big and sprawling any day.

Nat conducts detailed research on private online terrorist networks. He has several LLCs and S-Corps to his name, which he established by the time he was in his mid-20s.

He is also a frequent buyer on the dark marketplace of material nonpublic information, most of the time stolen by other hackers from law firms and banks. He uses this information in order to conduct a tidy one-man insider trading business. He buys the kind of data Bo used to provide on the dark web, discreetly.

Nat is one of the few people Bo keeps in touch with. Bo expects Nat will never get caught. Because unlike in the massive operation behind the hacks against NOW Bank, this Israeli is content with pocketing only a few million dollars here and there. Nat prefers to focus his life's work on hunting terrorists. He justifies his cybercrime by saying it helps fund this endeavor. Bo can't hold that kind of morality against him—it's a higher justification than his own ever was.

Still, Bo is glad to have moved on from that life. The indictments of Chinese and Israeli and Russian hackers remind him of the terrible end he may have had.

Bo is quietly dating someone. A trader from India. Very quietly, since same-sex relationships carry various legal penalties in Singapore. It is the only part of his life in which he regularly flaunts the law. Still, it is a quiet life. Just like his mother had always wanted for him.

He almost never thinks about his old life anymore. Blown off to a faraway desert, scattered for all time.

19.

The Long Trip

It's a rare night out for Charlie Mack. He's one finger into a large glass of scotch as he contemplates a *New York Times* article about the 2012 terrorist attacks on a CIA compound in Benghazi, Libya.

"Is this true? How about this?" The Midtown bar looks like a law library by the light of the iPhone his companion holds up for him to see.

"Sure," he says with a shrug. "It's plausible."

Not yes or no, but plausible.

"I left right before it happened," he reminds them when they push for details.

"Did you take any time off in between?" one of his colleagues asks.

"No." Sip. Silence.

For years, he traveled the world, performing an extremely dangerous job. It was, somehow at the same time, a fantasy that could only be dreamed up by a particularly creative schoolboy. He gambled in

Monaco on the company dime. Helped liberate firearms from Gaddafi's compound after the 2011 coup.

There are many people in the cybersecurity field who cross over, from the bad guy timeline to the good guy timeline. There are some who stay firmly in one timeline or the other. Charlie Mack is in the middle of a long, arduous trip on the good guy timeline, whether he likes it or not.

He shows off pictures of himself, which he's saved on his own iPhone, in fatigues, sporting a beard and a weed-wacker haircut, holding two enormous guns, which he says were taken off Gaddafi when he was captured. In another photograph, an African militant is presenting him with a sword, a gift of some kind. For what, Charlie won't say.

"It must be incredibly jarring to go from that to this," his colleagues say, fishing for more details. North African intrigue to a bank lawyer and dad. From canvas fatigues to wool crepe.

Charlie puts the iPhone away. His companions put their phones away, too. Sip.

"Thought it was time to finally make use of my law degree." He doesn't say he earned his degree at Harvard. He doesn't need to.

One of his drinking companions, a veteran of NOW Bank, recalls Charlie's first day at work. Charlie was introduced to a big group of cybersecurity executives as a former employee of the CIA. There was silence and tension in the room. Then one executive shouted out: "Culinary Institute of America?"

Laughs all around. Then and now.

Someone asks again when, exactly, he started at NOW Bank. Someone else asks about the military. Something happens, nobody is sure what, but before Charlie is able to answer they are talking about something else. The Vatican. Then Donald Trump. Then Bob Raykoff.

Because Charlie has distracted them. It's something he is exceedingly good at. Whenever the camera focuses on him, he bumps it away with a flick of his wrist, aiming its lens at someone else. Maybe even someone who isn't there.

Raykoff, for example.

They share stories about the executive and some of his most frustrating moments. They laugh. They get loud.

Then the conversation turns a fourth time, to a scandal making headlines: the saga of a well-known security software maker called Achinsk Antivirus, which is based in Minsk. The company is highly rated, supplying one of the best-reviewed antivirus products in the world.

Achinsk's software is in millions of companies and on hundreds of government servers. The company has a free product used by a significant number of small law firms, independent workers, and start-up tech companies. The company is suspected of providing a back door to hundreds of organizations to be used by the Russian government, something Achinsk continues to deny as it pushes its free products more fervently than ever.

Charlie Mack appears resigned to this reality, but the rest of the group is aghast. One by one, they recount companies and government agencies they've worked for that have used Achinsk software. They remember how deeply embedded it was into sensitive systems. They sober up a little, quiet down, as they come to the same grim conclusion that all security professionals do: we're fundamentally compromised down to the very bones of every single one of our computers. What this means, really, for the cybersecurity profession itself is not something that will be solved tonight by a handful of drunk, 30-something bankers.

Charlie shifts the conversation again. He asks about Caroline. He is genuinely sad. Since she left NOW Bank, he hasn't had a chance to see her.

The conversation continues without him. While they talk, he reaches for *The New York Times* and glances at the article on Benghazi.

Sip.

René is preparing to leave TechSolu. Sig instructs her to get a sandwich at Cafe Americain and take a taxi home. Detours along his suggested route might be dangerous, but she will make just one.

René walks down the stairs to the cafe. Henry is on her chest, sleeping contentedly. She buys two yogurts and two prepackaged fruit smoothies. They will be good for the train ride, and easy to carry.

She asks the teller for two bags and she splits up the food.

She walks out of Cafe Americain, stops in front of the store. She slightly loosens the strap on her carrier. Henry shifts and she catches him, dropping her cell phone on the ground, breaking it. "How clumsy of me," she says.

She ducks into the technology store next door. Points to a burner phone on the wall. Shows the cashier her broken phone. Plausible deniability if Sig happens to find out.

She hails a taxi and heads home. Her head is whirring, but it spins in only one direction.

Out.

René plans to go to Germany on an EU passport she got while in college. She knows Sig won't go back to Germany because of some legal trouble he's been in there.

At home, she packs Henry's diaper bag and the two bags from Cafe Americain. One will serve as her purse, the other for the food.

The diaper bag holds four outfits for Henry, one extra for her. She will put on two layers of clothes, so three outfits total. The $1,000 she has folded into a roll and put inside a tampon box.

René will breastfeed Henry to get him milk-drunk and tired, so he will sleep through these last few moments in Romania.

Sig arrives home earlier than expected, drunk. To her surprise, he tells her he is going back out for the evening. Investors from Vladivostok are in town.

He changes his clothes into something nicer looking. René busies herself around the house and keeps her head down.

"That's right, don't look at me," he mumbles on his way out, slamming the door behind him.

It is 9 p.m. She knows he will be gone the rest of the night.

She lines up everything she's prepared. The diaper bag, the two Cafe Americain bags, Henry's carrier. This is all she needs. Using the burner smartphone, she calls a local taxi service. One Sig never uses. Gives the neighbor's address.

She gathers Henry up into the carrier, puts on one of Sig's jackets, and tucks her hair up under the hood. The car arrives. She picks up her bags and leaves.

René sidesteps through the darkness and over a small fence, to make it appear as if she is coming from her neighbor's house.

There is no night train from Arnica Valka. So she asks the driver to take her all the way to Bucharest, a 2-hour, 30-minute drive that will cost $120. Her mother is ill, she tells him. It's an emergency. He asks her a few questions. She says she is tired and wants to sleep. He leaves her in peace. She is grateful for this.

In Bucharest, she buys a train ticket to Prague. From there, she intends to go to Berlin. *It's beautiful there, lots of big companies,* she thinks to herself.

The train trip will be 24 hours. She books a private overnight room. It has a seat and a fold-out twin bed. $200. She has the Bitcoin wallet address and her private keys memorized. She will tap into them once she's in Germany, though it might not be easy to turn the cryptocurrency into euros. She attempts to tackle the problem from the train.

The train has good Wi-Fi, which she uses with her burner to set up a business identity in Estonia shielding her own name. She creates a PayPal account. She's learned all this from the guys at TechSolu, idly discussing what they will do with their earnings. Someday she will thank them.

She does a test transfer from CEX.IO, a company that can cash out and transfer Bitcoin into PayPal accounts. She sees now, for the first time, that Sig had taken most of her stash. She isn't surprised. She is more surprised that he's left a fair amount, enough to get by for a year if she's frugal. She transfers the remaining funds to PayPal. The transaction, thanks to the privacy of the blockchain, will be untraceable.

Henry is easy. He sleeps, wakes, feeds, sleeps. The privacy of the private car is glorious.

Despite being up all night, René doesn't feel tired in the slightest, nor sad, nor scared. Her blood is pure adrenaline. The pain in her jaw is gone.

By 1 a.m. Bucharest time, she imagines Sig stumbling home. He won't notice they are gone until he wakes up. This scenario is keeping her on edge. Imagining those first moments when he realizes she's not there, has taken the money, and has left him for good.

Will he come after her?

She doesn't think so. Sig values control above all things. If he knows she is no longer susceptible to his influence, he will simply cease to care about her.

This is what she hopes.

20.

The Reason

"Valery Romanov? Don't know him. He's in prison, you say?"

"I was wondering if you had heard of him," the reporter asks.

Victor Tanninberg laughs. "Why would I hear of him? For the last time, I'm not a hacker!"

His reporter friend sits on the corner of the bed in his small house. But that's only because there is nowhere else to sit. Every square inch of his place is covered with computer parts and wires and tools. Fox News blares in the background.

"So let's go back to my original question then, because I'm writing a story on it. Is it possible to cut the brakes on a car remotely? To blow out the tires or depress the accelerator? Everyone says it's possible, but nobody can demonstrate it."

Victor sits in a dark corner of the room, next to a fat rabbit named Sam. Both like to be close to the air conditioner.

"Why would I do such a thing as cut brakes?" he says. "I would just lose customer."

"I'm not asking if you would do it. I'm asking if it's possible."

"Why would I want to put myself in this kind of risk?"

He gestures around the room. The reporter, named Frances, assumes he's referring to the overflowing stacks of computers when he adds, "And give up all this?"

His computers are not "computers" as a consumer might think of them. They are computers that control each car's engine. Each of them is the size of a small, thick textbook. Accordingly, some are even filed like books on a bookshelf. The rest are bursting out of drawers and piling up on the couch.

He doesn't like when the reporter calls him a hacker. He has a PhD in string theory, he likes to remind her.

The reporter was in a jam, so he sold her one of his hacked cars. A '99 Chevy Lumina, a used cop car that looked like it was beaten with golf clubs. It drives like a Porsche.

The reporter wants to talk to him about his business, but Victor keeps turning the conversation to Donald Trump. The man from Queens has turned into an obsession for Victor. He shows the reporter a detailed map on his laptop of precisely how Trump will win the election. She tells him he's crazy. Never gonna happen. He won't even win the primary, she says.

He gets annoyed. Trump will win Michigan, Florida, Ohio, and Pennsylvania, he insists.

"You will see."

She laughs.

The reporter has come out to New Jersey to find out if assassination by car hacking is possible. It's one of the perennial what-ifs that she gets asked about the most. A tall tale, heretofore theoretical, that everyone from military generals to cybersecurity PR flacks to sociopathic executives seem to hope is true. It's part of the greater collection of apocalyptic cyberliterature under the headline of "Cyber Pearl Harbor" or "Cyber 9/11."

Huge lie, she thinks. Thirty years of this lie and so little to show for it. A court of lies. A kingdom of lies.

Everyone wants to scare their bosses, to maximum effect. More fear equals a bigger budget to combat that fear when what they are really doing is stoking it. The reporter just wants an answer, for today anyway. Some proof that this one little hallmark of horrific cyberthreats is legitimate. And if it is, an explanation of how it can be pulled off.

"Sounds like beginning of conspiracy theory," Victor says, a wry grin on his face. "Diplomat A dies. Diplomat A's supporters say he was assassinated by unknowable person related to Politician B. Conspiracy theory remains in perpetuity, benefiting all." He lights a cigarette, a long Parliament. "Yes, it can be done. But who would want to do such a thing?"

The reporter's mind reels. "OK, wow. But how?"

He looks at her with eyes narrowed to tiny slits. "Too hard to explain."

"I'm serious, so you go in, the same way you would tweak the—I don't know—fuel pump output . . ."

"You don't know what you're talking about."

"No shit. So explain it to me so I can understand."

"Would you like me to explain to you string theory, too? Maybe before lunch? You won't have any hope of understanding that, either. This isn't even my field, not even close. Someone would have to understand the complexities of the entire car network. People like this exist, but these are not run-of-the-mill idiots on the internet. CIA, Russian intelligence, Mossad, this is very complicated. Probably easier to dangle diplomat over tank of sharks."

The reporter doesn't answer, hoping he will continue. Victor does not.

She tries to fill in the space with more questions. "But can't you do it remotely? As the car is passing by?"

He pulls a face—pure exasperation. He collapses his head and shoulders down. Rubs the area between his eyes. She reminds him how many people have written articles about the threats to our consumer products, that, wired as they are to the internet, they could be turned against us, to be used for terrorism.

"Not my thing. Why are you so worried about cars? I'm worried about the electric grid." But he just pets his rabbit and turns his attention to a Trump rally in Fort Lauderdale on Fox.

"Look at this man, he is an animal," he says, a bright smile on his face. "He will win, you will see."

The reporter has learned a lesson through these conversations, that the significant cyber incidents indeed don't happen without a person behind the scenes who has a deeply felt reason for inflicting pain. People need reasons to do what they do, and hackers are people. Money is the usual reason, followed by loyalty to country—like Russia's intelligence directorate—or loyalty to a cause, like the Izz ad-Din al-Qassam Cyber Fighters.

If the reason isn't money or identification with some type of faction, it could be simple curiosity or something equally unpredictable. There are people like Dieter, who have managed to turn their curiosity into a profession, but at that point, the motivation becomes money—at least, enough to make a living doing what one enjoys.

Victor has an important point. For so long, worries about the damage hacking may cause us have been pointless and arcane. Why would somebody bother hacking a pacemaker? Why would a foreign nation risk a kinetic, guns-blazing war by meddling with our power grid?

Victor knows it's not the grandiose plots and huge explosions that should concern us but the gentle tide of insecurity that has been rolling in for 20 years. The little bits of erosion that, over time, change absolutely everything. The slow march on our infrastructure, dams and electric grids and wireless fidelity, that has been underway for decades.

21.

The Spaniard

These days Dieter Reichlin is drinking coffee by the gallon. Sig Himelman's life has turned into a real-life soap opera. He is ashamed of himself, but he can't get enough.

It's the summer of 2016 and the Russians are pulling all kinds of crazy shit on the Americans. It's been a roller-coaster ride from Dieter's recliner in Helsinki.

Fucking bad passwords. That's how easy it is to break into an American political party, he muses. No problem for even a nontechnician.

Then there're the simmering resentments, the complacency of social media, the utter disregard for technical privacy, the racial issues, such an enticing treat for a good social engineer. A hot cauldron of fucked-upness that Dieter suspects will play out well after November, but, he is confident, there is no way Trump can win.

Dieter is trying to come up with a new topic for a Norwegian magazine for which he occasionally writes. He wants to take on the attacks by Anders Behring Breivik, but with a twist: cyberterrorism.

How the next mass attack may be carried out by cyber means. He doesn't know where to start. For one thing, it's not terribly feasible, but the assignment is high profile and he wants to make it work.

So he procrastinates by flipping open his window into Sig's world, where something weird is unfolding. Something far more interesting. Something that started early in the morning yesterday, even earlier in Romanian time.

Sig has been using a tracking service to ping a cell phone, then a computer. It's unclear if they belong to Sig, and Dieter is intrigued momentarily. Both keep coming back with the location right there in Arnica Valka. Then silence for one hour.

Then Sig tries logging into a Bitcoin wallet. The balance is zero. Silence for another hour.

Then chaos. Twenty email messages, some of them checking on business deals. Others plying new women from Craigslist. Lonely hearts stuff. Sig is going above and beyond his usual charm, and all before 8 a.m.

Then Sig creates a new email address, HRH13023@romamail.ro. Then a message to an email address Dieter hadn't yet seen. One that makes him sit up in his seat.

R.Kreutz@ram.college.ro

I don't know where you are but please I beg that you forgive me. I don't know why you would leave but I am so worried about you and about dear Henry. You both are everything to me. I am not upset. I love you. Please come back and things can be the way they were.

Dieter leans back in his seat. René Kreutz. Henry. Things had just taken an unexpected turn to say the least.

He thinks for a while. Walks to the fridge and grabs a tomato sandwich. Thankfully there is some egg salad left from the previous evening. He piles that on top of the sandwich, making a small mountain. He puts on another pot of coffee before going back to the Sig Himelman show.

Next Sig creates another new email address. RomanianLad991@ romamail.ro. He uses this to email what appears to be another lonely heart from Craigslist.

I am terribly sorry to hear what happened to you in Marrakesh in 2011. You can email me here from now on at my real address. I have a good friend, a Russian friend, who was injured in the same blast, if you can believe it! I know you are Muslim and so are probably not interested in a man like me, someone who is not Muslim. But you are so beautiful. And so pure. So divine. I have spent the past week thinking of nothing but you. It's hard to work, hard to even think clearly. I think the fact that my friend was injured there and you are too is a sign that God is bringing us together. God or Allah or however we refer to Him at a given moment.

I know somebody who could help get you a passport here. As I said, I own a successful company and I am looking for a secretary. But more importantly, I am looking for a companion, someone to share my big house with, spend money on. Somebody to love and who will love me in return. I have had a hard life too, but that makes times like these even sweeter. I have been unlucky in love. I was scammed by my last wife, she stole so much money from me. But I have hope that someone as pure as you could bless my life and change these views.

It's so bizarre. Dieter can't quite make sense of what is happening. "Did you pile egg salad on top of that?" his wife's voice intrudes on his spying. "That's not how it's supposed to work. Mikael Blom-kvist would never do that." She is referring to the male, middle-aged hero from *The Girl with the Dragon Tattoo*.

"Blomkvist? No, no, no, I am Lisbeth Salander!" Dieter sucks in his stomach in imitation of the novel's slender young female hero and hacker extraordinaire.

"You couldn't hack your way out of a paper bag. And you've got-ten fat on top of it."

Dieter smiles, aware as he is that sharp barbs like this mean sex might be around the corner. It adds another level of intrigue to this strange morning.

"Well," he says, choosing his words carefully, "you're an accoun-tant. You're not even part of the narrative."

His wife throws her head back and feigns laughter. A hearty do-not-wake-the-babies laugh.

"Read this," he says.

She does. He has shared with her many iterations of the Sig show, of which she disapproves. She sips her coffee again. Raises her eye-brows dismissively.

"Typical. Dangerous for her, if her passport is on the line. He got her involved in his illegal shit, then tied her down with a baby. That's ter-rorism. Of the domestic type. Imagine what else he feels entitled to?"

She gets up. One of the children is calling for her. She flicks her nearly white hair in his direction as she walks away.

Dieter is satisfied. He has an answer. He has his thesis for his ar-ticle. And he will be having sex tonight.

René doesn't sleep until they get to Munich. They stopped once in Hungary. She has never been there and has always wanted to visit. She believes, but can't recall for certain, that she has family here.

She looks everywhere for Sig. But he is nowhere. He's sent a message to her email address, a short one. She ignores it.

In Munich, it's nighttime again. They have been traveling for 24 hours. Henry is bubbly and talkative in his carrier. It's much colder here, so she buys him a cap with some of her remaining cash. She briefly considers finding a hotel, but something tells her to keep going. She doesn't like the weather. The people look too straitlaced. She imagines they can tell she's a criminal. She sees the next train from Munich terminates in Malaga, Spain.

Probably warmer there. She speaks some Spanish. It's close to Gibraltar, she knows. A tax haven. So probably some criminals around. She wonders if she will always only be comfortable in the company of criminals.

She tries to ask the teller in German whether it's nice in Malaga this time of year. The teller answers her in English. "Oh, I believe it's to be twenty-one degrees Celsius and sunny tomorrow."

Malaga it is.

22.

The Project Manager

In Malaga, René Kreutz finds a one-bedroom attic apartment. It's modest, but has a beautiful deck with flowers and sunset views. The house is owned by a Muslim family too busy with their own children to pay any attention to what she and Henry are doing.

She starts applying for jobs. She withdraws little bits of the Bitcoin money at a time. She keeps to herself. Talks to no one.

The sun begins to thaw her out, though. By September 2016, she is more open. She leaves the house more often, starts to recognize the faces in her neighborhood, and even brings Henry down to the beach. It's hard to find a job. Spain is in a recession. But she has enough to get by for a year if she absolutely has to.

Every so often, the couple who own the house—Norah and Muhammad—leave her meals by the door, cookies; at Ramadan, whole servings of kebabs and salad and soup. On one of these occasions, they run into each other. She invites them onto the balcony for a conversation.

They ask why she came to Spain. She tells them that she came here for the sun and the weather, that she and Henry were getting sick with allergies and colds back in Bucharest and she needed a change. She's hoping to finish college, which she started back home. Hopes to find a job soon. Something in technology. She has a background in it, she tells them, but on the support side, she is not a technologist.

"What company was it?" Muhammad asks.

She hesitates, not having meant to let her guard down with anyone, and nervously blurts out, "TechSolu."

"I've never heard of it." She feels some relief. "What kind of company?"

"Ransomware. Mitigation," she says, taking a sip of water. "I mostly did customer service, to be honest."

"Any project management? My brother works at Insite—have you heard of it? They have a technology office here."

René has heard of it. It is based in Silicon Valley and is one of the biggest technology companies in the world.

"I think I know somebody there," René says, the evening Malaga breeze making her a little careless. "But that was a long time ago."

"Well, if you want to put together a resume, I'll send it to him. They're desperate for project managers. And the ransomware thing—I'm sure they'll be interested. Good place for moms to work—they love women!"

Norah gives her husband a sideward glance, a hand motion to settle down.

René hasn't heard from Sig since the email he sent in March. She nods and smiles. "I will. I'll do it right away."

Caroline Chan and Charlie Mack and Bob Raykoff and Joe the Kool-Aid Man and Carl Ramirez, who is still in Singapore, and Bo Chou, who is also in Singapore, and the reporter who is friends with Victor and everyone else who ever worked in cybersecurity at NOW Bank have been reading every last bit of information they can get their hands on about the Venice hackers now that an indictment has been issued.

The FBI has been quiet about its progress, hasn't spoken to anybody about what was happening. Then, suddenly, the indictments. Two Israelis, Yuval Dev and Ivan Misrachi; one Russian Israeli, Leonid Kravitz; and a money launderer named Tony Belvedere.

The information they were stealing, the allegations maintain, was being used for a pump-and-dump scheme. For most of the people following the case, it's the first time they've seen all of the details pulled together in one place, even though they were intimately involved in what happened.

Two of the alleged conspirators are picked up in December 2016. The indictment outlines the numerous other banks, software companies, and newspapers that were hacked at the same time. The perpetrators had 100 million names to work with.

The ringleader, Dev, used the information to contact his customers and try to offload certain stocks in an effort to manipulate the securities market.

The trail goes well beyond the relatively simple, straightforward cybercrime that Caroline and her compatriots were fighting in the summer of 2014.

In particular, between approximately 2007 and July 2015, Dev owned and operated unlawful internet gambling businesses in the United States and abroad; owned and operated multinational payment processors for illegal pharmaceutical suppliers, counterfeit and malware distributors, and unlawful internet casinos; and owned and controlled Coin.mx, an illegal United States-based Bitcoin exchange that operated in violation of federal anti-money laundering laws.

Dev earned hundreds of millions this way. He concealed $100 million, at least, in Swiss banks and other places across the globe, within 75 shell companies, in brokerage accounts. He even stashed some of it in asset management accounts, maybe at NOW Bank. Dev and his compatriots used 200 different aliases and 30 false passports issued from 16 different countries.

Dev bragged about his exploits, the government says. "We buy stocks very cheap, perform machinations, then play with them. Buying stocks in the U.S.—it's like drinking freaking vodka in Russia."

Dev would call and lie to people whose personal information he'd stolen. Like Bo, Dev would lie about where the information came from and claim he got it from a publicly available "investors' database."

In emails, Dev would discuss the low risk of law enforcement intervention. Like Valery Romanov before him, he wasn't afraid of the authorities until he had a reason to be.

"In Israel, you guys probably don't have to be afraid of the USA, meaning that even if there is some case, they won't be able to do anything?" Belvedere asked him in one exchange, to which Dev replied: "There is nothing to be afraid of in Israel."

Then the conspiracy hatched another type of scheme: market manipulation of a different sort—insider trading.

"The top managers at NOW Bank, they have some interesting information in their email? Regarding working on the stock market, etcetera? It's a big company, after all. Maybe they have some secrets. What do you think?" asked Leonid Kravitz.

"Yes, this is a very cool idea," Dev responded. "We need to think how we can do it."

23

The Reporter

Bo Chou clicks his tongue repeatedly. A reporter who was introduced to him 10 years ago at a convention in Shanghai asks him questions about the Dev indictment.

How she's managed to stay in touch with him for so long, he doesn't know. But he does know she's perpetually barking up the wrong tree. She reads back the names and the statements obtained by the Department of Justice. She wants to know what he thinks.

"These people, they're terrible," he says. "Listen, do you know anyone at Google? I'm really interested in making some contacts there."

"If I knew anyone at Google, I wouldn't be doing this job," she says.

"I really can't help you," Bo says. "Sorry. I don't know anybody who has ever worked on one of these types of schemes, come on. I don't know anything about insider trading. No, no, can't help, sorry."

He hangs up. He'll talk more to her later, when he's not at work. Bo now lives in a world that is colorful, specifically Red, Amber, and Green. This RAG status, the term that defines how well a project is proceeding, is the ever-present code of the project manager. Red is bad; Amber is kind of bad; Green is good.

But right now, he has a project that is in red status at the hedge fund where he works that he needs to clean up. His mom's birthday is tomorrow, and he wants to get her a card before the stores close. His official title is project manager. His projects are insider threats. His job is to manage them.

And he manages the shit out of them.

Dieter has not lost track of Sig, but his activities have become tedious and a little sad. Sig's business operation seems to have fallen apart. Things never panned out with the girl from Marrakesh.

Surprisingly, Sig has suddenly lost interest in pursuing women. Now he is corresponding with other criminals about setting up a crypto-mining operation.

Cryptomining involves using, or stealing, the power generated by computers—which is the basis for cryptocurrencies like Bitcoin. In order to do this on a large scale, individuals put a relatively benign type of malware on computers belonging to other people. It involves no phone calls, no personal contact at all, and generates passive income while the criminal sleeps.

Passive aggressive. Suits Sig well, Dieter thinks.

Dieter never published his paper on terrorism. The magazine editor thought his angle on the recurrent themes of entitlement among cy-berterrorists was too "fluffy."

He sends it to a journalist he knows through his professional network to get her opinion. She takes forever to get back to him. Her newspaper doesn't take submissions, she replies, rudely.

She calls him later to apologize. Says she has some other questions for him, about Romania and ransomware.

He doesn't trust journalists much. He weighs whether to talk to her. When it comes to Sig, he doesn't expect he'll ever see him again.

He destroys the malware he planted on Sig's computer, losing his cousin to the ether.

Hands off. Sig just wants to be hands off. Passive income is better than anything active. Bitcoin could spike soon. He's got a lot of it. And he wants more.

Mikael Gunther is the first and last remaining TechSolu employee; everyone else has left. Some of them wondered what happened to René. Sig told them she ran off with another man, the bitch. One of them wondered out loud if he'd killed her. Then they'd all slowly faded away, to other enterprises. Whether they were criminal or legit, no one would say.

With cryptomining, it is all passive. Mikael showed him how to infect remote computers. Control them like a botnet, but all they do is produce the energy required to create more cryptocurrency. There are new types each day. If they exploit whole databases, like the big data centers Insite is setting up in Poland, they will be rich.

If they can co-opt some of that power, they'll have Bitcoin flowing like water along the Danube.

René reviews the project manager job description that Muhammad had sent to her. It's filled with incomprehensible jargon and technological speak.

There's tons of stuff about cloud servers and red-amber-green status and other protocols typically followed by corporate project executives.

Must have a PMP or related certificate, a reference to certifications typically held by project managers, which René does not have. *AB-*

SOLUTELY MUST have a CISSP or CERM, referring to cybersecurity certifications that René also does not have.

MUST understand Python, a reference to a computer coding language that René does not understand.

She thinks there is no way this will work out. Then the last bullet point gives her some hope:

MUST be a PowerPoint NINJA.

Henry is sleeping in his stroller. This is how she gets him to settle down every evening. She types with two hands and pushes the stroller with her foot back and forth, back and forth.

She glances over at him. Makes a small karate-chop motion. *Ninja*.

She takes her meager resume, filled with holes and half-truths, and puts it into a PowerPoint. She does graphics and sweeping transitions from page to page. She adds subtle but unique shadings and color. She enhances graphics to support the best possible readability. She submits it to both the recruiter and the executive listed on the job description as hiring for the role.

The next day, the recruiter calls her and says she doesn't have enough experience for the job.

Five minutes later, the executive in charge of hiring calls her, too.

"Listen, can you do presentations like that PowerPoint all the time? This is amazing. Is this what you can do?"

René smiles. She knows by the sound of his voice that she has him. A throwback to her previous life. She answers in the affirmative. Breezes through a description of her experience in ransomware mitigation.

"That's interesting, we haven't had a very big problem with ransomware."

"Oh really?"

"But managing the problem, as a project manager, that is what we're looking for. From a project management standpoint. We need to set up a disaster recovery plan for ransomware; that's something you could help with, I'm sure."

"I can definitely do that, sir."

"All right, let me call the recruiter and tell them. Sorry, they're not always on the same page as us."

After several months, René is thriving in her new job. Her manager is even sending her to a conference in New York. Henry will stay with Muhammad and Norah and their kids for two days while she is gone. It's the first time they will be separated. Her manager warns her there will be reporters at the conference and so she should be careful who she talks to. She always is, she replies.

It's May 2017, and it's hot and gorgeous in Malaga. It's going to be Mother's Day in America on Sunday, and René has gotten herself and Henry a little cake to celebrate.

But that Saturday, a global, sweeping ransomware attack called Wanna-Cry hits everyone where it hurts.

Including Insite.

As René is inundated with images and emails about the attack, she sees a few screenshots that—though unrelated to WannaCry—echo some designs from her previous life. She is unstirred.

But the fallout from the event is sensational. Pictures of stopped am-bulances in the United Kingdom, offices shut down across Europe, panicked security personnel in the United States. Now everyone in the world knows what ransomware is, though this attack has no re-semblance to any of the work TechSolu ever did.

Still, the conditions are just right for a ransomware specialist's star to shine. René does what René does best: she shines.

It's a hot day in Queens. A prelude to a muggy Mother's Day. Victor Tanninberg is cranky as hell. A gastrointestinal issue has flared up.

He spent the last week getting into vicious arguments with his doctor over the matter. He has intensely researched gastrointestinal issues. His doctor, he says, is a fucking idiot blinded by the tyranny of treatments preferred by the healthcare companies.

Although he'd rather be home, he's come to Queens to fix the reporter's car. She gets a text from her former colleague, Caroline, about the attack they're calling WannaCry, and it distracts her.

He has a can of coolant in one hand, an iced tea with extra sugar in the other. The reporter is making spaghetti. It's Mother's Day.

"I'm going to write a book about hackers," she says. "I want to put you in it. What do you think?"

"I'm not a fucking hacker. We've discussed this."

"You say you're not a car mechanic, either. But here you are, fixing my car," she says, and smiles.

"Well, I'm tired of that, too," he says, smiling.

There is no profession on earth Victor despises more than journalism. The two of them have been arguing about the elections for the past hour. Now some sort of ransomware attack is breaking out and she says she might have to cut the visit short.

"I don't want to be in any book," he tells her.

"But what would I call you if you were?"

He does not hesitate.

"Victor Tanninberg."

Epilogue

We Didn't Start the Fire

I'm sitting at my desk at *The Wall Street Journal*, getting ready to print out my letter of resignation, when I decide it will be easier and more efficient to email it instead.

I hit send. I'm sad. It was a dream job, combining my experience in the field and my writing ability to provide greater insight and nuance to reporting on hackers.

But it's just not working out.

I check my voicemail. There are 10 calls, and the first seven are from PR specialists pitching insidious dark web finds.

"You may have heard of ransomware," one of them starts. I delete it.

Then number eight. It's an autistic Billy Joel fanatic, one of my many oddball sources, who somehow has caught wind that I'm having job trouble. Anthony is one of several sources for whom I only have a screen name.

He's taken the time to write and sing a technology version of Billy Joel's "We Didn't Start the Fire" in a bid to cheer me up.

It's bad. But it works. And for a computer geek, Anthony's got some surprisingly good pipes:

NBS, John Curtiss, Math Lab, New Census
Lanczos, Krylov, Hestenes and Stiefel
SEAC, UNIVAC, FBI and Fingerprints
Brooks Act, MAGIC Facts, Churchill Eisenhart
FIPS 1, CST, Railroad Club at MIT
Vote Counts, Jargon File, Linux Kernel One,
Bill Joy, Larry Wall, Linus, Guido van Rossum
Captain Crunch, Ma Bell, Twenty-Six Hundred[1]
We didn't start the fire
It was always burning, since the world's been turning

It goes on like this for several verses. Anthony wends his way through the history of Captain Crunch, the Cuckoo's Egg, the Morris worm, Winn Schwartau and the cyber Pearl Harbor, Stuxnet, Shamoon, ransomware, Equifax.

The song ends at the then-hinted-at indictment of 12 Russians for disrupting the 2016 presidential election.

This is an apt time for a reminder of how big this sea of knowledge is. How incredibly vast the universe of cybersecurity has become. How insignificant I am within it. How little I should care about my transient work problems.

After this foray into journalism, I had wanted to go back to a career in cybersecurity, but I took a job at CNBC instead. I don't know what to expect. The stock market is a little foreign to me. Why would I do

---

1. See Appendix B for a full interpretation.

such a thing when all I want to do is sit in a back office somewhere and trade stories with other nerds?

My cell buzzes. I have an incoming, encrypted text from somebody called "the Bucharest bunny." That's enough of an answer for now.

I suppose there are a few more stories to tell.

Appendix A

Glossary of Cyberterms

Adapted for this book from the National Initiative for Cybersecurity Careers and Studies, a division of the Department of Homeland Security.

ADVERSARY: An individual, group, organization, or government that conducts, or has the intent to conduct, detrimental activities.

AIR GAP: To physically separate or isolate a system from other systems or networks (verb). The physical separation or isolation of a system from other systems or networks (noun).

ALERT: A notification that a specific attack has been detected or directed at an organization's information systems.

ANTIVIRUS SOFTWARE: A program that monitors a computer or network to detect or identify major types of malicious code and to prevent or contain malware incidents, sometimes by removing or neutralizing the malicious code.

ASSET: A person, structure, facility, or material that has value. Can also apply to digital information, records, and resources, or abstract processes, relationships, and reputations. Anything that contributes to the success of something, such as an organizational mission; assets are things of value or properties to which value can be assigned.

ATTACK: An attempt to gain unauthorized access to system services, resources, or information, or an attempt to compromise system integrity. The intentional act of attempting to bypass one or more security services or controls of an information system.

AUTHENTICATION: The process of verifying the identity or other attributes of an entity (user, process, or device).

Also the process of verifying the source and integrity of data.

BLACKLIST: A list of entities that are blocked or denied privileges or access.

BOT: A computer connected to the internet that has been surreptitiously and/or secretly compromised with malicious code to perform activities under the command and control of a remote administrator. A member of a larger collection of compromised computers known as a botnet.

BOTNET: A collection of computers compromised by malicious code and controlled across a network.

BUG: An unexpected and relatively small defect, fault, flaw, or imperfection in an information system or device.

CLOUD COMPUTING: A model for enabling on-demand network access to a shared pool of configurable computing capabilities or resources (e.g., networks, servers, storage, applications, and services) that can be rapidly provisioned and released with minimal management effort or service provider interaction.

CRITICAL INFRASTRUCTURE: The systems and assets, whether physical or virtual, so vital to an organization or nation-state that the incapacity or destruction of such may have a debilitating impact on the security, economy, public health or safety, environment, or any combination of these matters.

CRYPTOGRAPHY: The use of mathematical techniques to provide security services, such as confidentiality, data integrity, entity authentication, and data origin authentication. The art and science concerning the principles, means, and methods for converting plaintext into ciphertext and for restoring encrypted ciphertext to plaintext.

CYBERINFRASTRUCTURE: Any electronic information and communications system and its services, and the information contained therein. The information and communications systems and services composed of all hardware and software that process, store, and communicate information, or any combination of these elements.

CYBEROPERATIONS: Cybersecurity work in which a person (1) performs activities to gather evidence about criminal or foreign intelligence entities in order to mitigate possible or real-time threats, (2) protects against espionage or insider threats, foreign sabotage, international terrorist activities, and/or (3) supports other intelligence activities.

CYBERSECURITY: The activity, process, ability, capability, or state whereby information and communications systems, and the information contained therein, are protected from and/or defended against damage, unauthorized use or modification, or exploitation. Also pertains to the strategy, policy, and standards regarding the security of and operations in cyberspace, and encompasses the full range of threat reduction, vulnerability reduction, deterrence, international engagement, incident response, resiliency, and recovery policies and activities, including computer network operations, information assurance, law enforcement, diplomacy, military, and intelligence missions as they relate to the security and stability of the global information and communications infrastructure.

CYBERSPACE: The interdependent network of information technology infrastructures that includes the internet, telecommunications networks, computer systems, and embedded processors and controllers.

DATA BREACH: The unauthorized movement or disclosure of sensitive information to a party, usually outside the organization, that is not authorized to have or see the information. Related terms: data loss, exfiltration

DATA INTEGRITY: The property that data is complete, intact, and trusted and has not been modified or destroyed in an unauthorized or accidental manner.

DATA LOSS: The result of unintentionally or accidentally deleting data, forgetting where it is stored, or it being exposed to an unauthorized party.

DATA LOSS PREVENTION: A set of procedures and mechanisms to stop sensitive data from leaving a security boundary.

DATA MINING: The process or techniques used to analyze large sets of existing information to discover previously unrevealed patterns or correlations.

DECRYPTING: The process of transforming ciphertext into its original plaintext. The process of converting encrypted data back into its original form, so it can be understood. Synonyms: decoding, deciphering

DENIAL OF SERVICE (DOS): An attack that prevents or impairs the authorized use of information system resources or services.

DIGITAL FORENSICS: The processes and specialized techniques for gathering, retaining, and analyzing system-related data (digital evidence) for investigative purposes. Synonyms: computer forensics, forensics

DISTRIBUTED DENIAL OF SERVICE (DDOS): A denial of service technique that uses numerous systems to perform the attack simultaneously.

ENCRYPTION: The process of transforming plaintext into ciphertext. Converting data into a form that cannot be easily understood by unauthorized people.

ENTERPRISE RISK MANAGEMENT: A comprehensive approach to risk management that engages people, processes, and systems across an organization to improve the quality of decision-making for managing risks that may hinder an organization's ability to achieve its objectives. May also involve identifying mission dependencies on enterprise capabilities, identifying and prioritizing risks due to defined threats, implementing countermeasures to provide both a static risk posture and an effective dynamic response to active threats, and assessing enterprise performance against threats and adjusting countermeasures as necessary.

EVENT: An observable occurrence in an information system or network. Something that provides an indication that an incident is occurring or at least raises the suspicion that an incident may be occurring.

EXFILTRATION: The unauthorized transfer of information from an information system.

EXPLOIT: A technique to breach the security of a network or information system in violation of security policy.

EXPOSURE: The condition of being unprotected, thereby allowing access to information or capabilities that an attacker can use to enter a system or network.

FIREWALL: A capability to limit network traffic between networks and/or information systems. A hardware/software device or software program that limits network traffic according to a set of rules of what access is and is not allowed or authorized.

HACKER: An unauthorized user who attempts to gain or gains access to an information system.

HASHING: A process of applying a mathematical algorithm against a set of data to produce a numeric value (a "hash value") that represents the data.

IDENTITY AND ACCESS MANAGEMENT: The methods and processes used to manage subjects and their authentication and authorizations to access specific objects.

IMPACT: The consequence of an action.

INCIDENT: An occurrence that actually or potentially results in adverse effects on or poses a threat to an information system or the information that the system processes, stores, or transmits, and that may require a response action to mitigate the consequences. An occurrence that constitutes a violation or imminent threat of violation of security policies, security procedures, or acceptable use policies.

INCIDENT MANAGEMENT: The management and coordination of activities associated with an actual or potential occurrence of an event that may result in adverse consequences to information or information systems.

INCIDENT RESPONSE: The activities that address the short-term, direct effects of an incident and may also support short-term recovery. Cybersecurity work where a person: responds to crises or urgent situations within the pertinent domain to mitigate immediate and potential threats; uses mitigation, preparedness, and response and recovery approaches, as needed, to maximize survival of life, preservation of property, and information security.

INDUSTRIAL CONTROL SYSTEM: An information system used to control industrial processes such as manufacturing, product handling, production, and distribution or to control infrastructure assets.

INFORMATION ASSURANCE: The measures that protect and defend information and information systems by ensuring their availability, integrity, and confidentiality.

INFORMATION TECHNOLOGY: Any equipment or interconnected system or subsystem of equipment that processes, transmits, receives, or interchanges data or information.

INSIDER THREAT: A person or group of persons within an organization who pose a potential risk through violating security policies. One or more individuals with the access to and/or inside knowledge of a company, organization, or enterprise that would allow them to exploit the vulnerabilities of that entity's security, systems, services, products, or facilities with the intent to cause harm.

INTEGRITY: The property whereby information, an information system, or a component of a system has not been modified or destroyed in an unauthorized manner. A state in which information has remained unaltered from the point it was produced by a source, during transmission, storage, and eventual receipt by the destination.

INTRUSION: An unauthorized act of bypassing the security mechanisms of a network or information system.

INTRUSION DETECTION: The process and methods for analyzing information from networks and information systems to determine if a security breach has occurred.

INVESTIGATION: A systematic and formal inquiry into a qualified threat or incident using digital forensics and/or other traditional criminal inquiry techniques to determine the events that transpired and to collect evidence. Any cybersecurity work in which a person applies tactics, techniques, and procedures for a full range of investigative tools and processes, including interview and interrogation techniques, surveillance, countersurveillance, and surveillance detection, and appropriately evaluates the benefits of prosecution versus intelligence gathering.

KEY: The numerical value used to control cryptographic operations, such as decryption, encryption, signature generation, or signature verification.

KEYLOGGER: Software or hardware that tracks keystrokes and keyboard events, usually to monitor actions by the user of an information system.

KEY PAIR: A public key and its corresponding private key. Two mathematically related keys having the property that one key can be used to encrypt a message that can only be decrypted using the other key.

MALICIOUS CODE: Program code intended to perform an unauthorized function or process that will have adverse impact on the confidentiality, integrity, or availability of an information system.

MALWARE: Software that compromises the operation of a system by performing an unauthorized function or process. Synonyms: malicious code, malicious applet, malicious logic.

MITIGATION: The application of one or more measures to reduce the likelihood of an unwanted occurrence and/or lessen its consequences. Can also involve implementing appropriate risk-reduction controls based on risk management priorities and analysis of alternatives.

OUTSIDER THREAT: A person or group of persons external to an organization who are not authorized to access its assets and pose a potential risk to the organization and its assets.

PACKETS: Packets, or network packets, consist of data, formatted to be carried over a network, typically including information about controls and end users.

When a website receives too many packets at once, it can become unbalanced, resulting in a crash of the website or a takeover of the website by a malicious actor.

PASSIVE ATTACK: An actual assault perpetrated by an intentional threat source that attempts to learn or make use of information from a system but does not attempt to alter the system, its resources, its data, or its operations.

PASSWORD: A string of characters (letters, numbers, and/or other symbols) used to authenticate an identity or to verify access authorization.

PENETRATION: Intrusion into a network or system.

PEN TEST: A colloquial term for penetration test or penetration testing.

PENETRATION TESTING: An evaluation methodology whereby assessors search for vulnerabilities and attempt to circumvent the security features of a network and/or information system.

PERSONAL IDENTIFYING INFORMATION/PERSONALLY IDENTIFIABLE INFORMATION: The information that permits the identity of an individual to be directly or indirectly inferred.

PHISHING: A digital form of social engineering to deceive individuals into providing sensitive information.

PRIVACY: The assurance that the confidentiality of and access to certain information about an entity is protected. The ability of individuals to understand and exercise control over how information about themselves may be used by others.

PRIVATE KEY: A cryptographic key that must be kept confidential and is used to enable the operation of an asymmetric cryptographic algorithm. The secret part of an asymmetric key pair that is uniquely associated with an entity.

PUBLIC KEY: A cryptographic key that may be widely published and is used to enable the operation of an asymmetric cryptographic algorithm. The public part of an asymmetric key pair that is uniquely associated with an entity.

PUBLIC KEY CRYPTOGRAPHY: A branch of cryptography in which a cryptographic system or algorithm uses two uniquely linked keys: a public key and a private key (a key pair).

RECOVERY: The activities after an incident or event to restore essential services and operations in the short and medium term and to fully restore all capabilities in the longer term.

RED TEAM: A group authorized and organized to emulate a potential adversary's attack or exploitation capabilities against an enterprise's cybersecurity posture.

REDUNDANCY: Additional or alternative systems, subsystems, assets, or processes that maintain a degree of overall functionality in case of loss or failure of another system, subsystem, asset, or process.

RESILIENCE: The ability to adapt to changing conditions and prepare for, withstand, and rapidly recover from disruption.

RESPONSE: The activities that address the short-term, direct effects of an incident and may also support short-term recovery.

RISK ASSESSMENT: The product or process that collects information and assigns values to risks for the purpose of setting priorities, developing or comparing courses of action, and informing decision-making. The appraisal of the risks facing an entity, asset, system, or network, organizational operations, individuals, geographic areas, other organizations, or society, including determining the extent to which adverse circumstances or events could result in harmful consequences.

RISK MANAGEMENT: The process of identifying, analyzing, assessing, and communicating risk and accepting, avoiding, transferring, or controlling it to an acceptable level considering associated costs and benefits of any actions taken. These actions may include (1) conducting a risk assessment; (2) implementing strategies to mitigate risks; (3) continuously monitoring risk over time; and (4) documenting the overall risk management program.

ROOTKIT: A set of software tools with administrator-level access privileges installed on an information system and designed to hide the presence of the tools, maintain the access privileges, and conceal the activities conducted by the tools.

SECURITY PROGRAM MANAGEMENT OR PROJECT MANAGEMENT: Work where a person manages information security implications within the organization, a specific program, or other area of responsibility, to include strategic, personnel, infrastructure, policy enforcement, emergency planning, security awareness, and other resources.

SIGNATURE: A recognizable, distinguishing pattern.

SITUATIONAL AWARENESS: Comprehending information about the current and developing security posture and risks based on information gathered, observation, analysis, knowledge, and/or experience. In cybersecurity, comprehending the current status and security posture with respect to availability, confidentiality, and integrity of networks, systems, users, and data, as well as projecting future states of these.

SOFTWARE ASSURANCE: The level of confidence that software is free from vulnerabilities, either intentionally designed into the software or accidentally inserted at any time during its life cycle, and that the software functions in the intended manner.

SPAM: The abuse of electronic messaging systems to indiscriminately send unsolicited bulk messages.

SPOOFING: Faking the sending address of a transmission to gain illegal or unauthorized entry into a secure system. The deliberate inducement of a user or resource to take incorrect action. Impersonating, masquerading, piggybacking, and mimicking are forms of spoofing.

SPYWARE: Software that is secretly or surreptitiously installed into an information system without the knowledge of the system user or owner.

SUPPLY CHAIN: A system of organizations, people, activities, information, and resources for creating and moving products, including product components and/or services from suppliers, to their customers.

SYSTEM ADMINISTRATOR: The person who installs, configures, troubleshoots, and maintains server configurations (hardware and software) to ensure their confidentiality, integrity, and availability. Also manages accounts, firewalls, and patches and is responsible for access control, passwords, and account creation and administration.

TABLETOP EXERCISE: A discussion-based exercise where personnel meet in a classroom setting or breakout groups and are presented with a scenario to validate the content of plans, procedures, policies, cooperative agreements, or other information for managing an incident.

THREAT: A circumstance or event that indicates the potential to exploit vulnerabilities and to adversely impact organizational operations, organizational assets, including information and information systems, individuals, other organizations, or society. May include an individual or group of individuals, an entity such as an organization, or a nation, action, or occurrence.

THREAT ACTOR: An individual, group, organization, or government that conducts or has the intent to conduct detrimental activities.

THREAT ANALYSIS: The detailed evaluation of the characteristics of individual threats. Cybersecurity work that includes identifying and assessing the capabilities and activities of cybercriminals or foreign intelligence entities and producing findings to help initialize or support law enforcement and counterintelligence investigations or activities.

THREAT ASSESSMENT: The product or process of identifying or evaluating entities, actions, or occurrences, whether natural or man-made, that have or indicate the potential to harm life, information, operations, and/or property.

TICKET: In access control, data that authenticates the identity of a client or a service and, together with a temporary encryption key (a session key), forms a credential.

TRAFFIC LIGHT PROTOCOL: A set of designations employing four colors (red, amber, green, and white) used to ensure that sensitive information is shared with the correct audience.

TROJAN HORSE: A computer program that appears to have a useful function but also has a hidden and potentially malicious function that evades security mechanisms, sometimes by exploiting legitimate authorizations of a system entity that invokes the program.

UNAUTHORIZED ACCESS: Any access that violates the stated security policy.

VIRUS: A computer program that can replicate itself, infect a computer without user permission or knowledge, and then spread or propagate to another computer.

VULNERABILITY: A characteristic or specific weakness that renders an organization or asset open to exploitation by a given threat or susceptible to a given hazard.

WEAKNESS: A shortcoming or imperfection in software code, design, architecture, or deployment that, under proper conditions, could become a vulnerability or contribute to the introduction of vulnerabilities.

WHITELIST: A list of entities that are considered trustworthy and are granted access or privileges.

WORM: A self-replicating, self-propagating, self-contained program that uses networking mechanisms to spread itself.

Appendix B

Epilogue Explained

NBS, JOHN CURTISS, MATH LAB, NEW CENSUS

In 1901, Congress created the National Bureau of Standards (**NBS**), which would later turn into the National Institute for Standards in Technology, the organization that would create the country's primary framework for cybersecurity. Throughout the 1930s and 1940s, NBS produced the "math tables project," a division of Roosevelt's Works Projects Administration, which led to some of the foundational mathematics for today's internet.

John Curtiss—a pioneer in "the salt mines of computing"—came up with some of the first computational algorithms associated with modern computing. Curtiss helped found the Applied **Mathematics Lab**oratories, which would become the U.S.-based Applied Mathematics Division of the U.S. Department of Energy's Office of Science. It would ultimately develop some of the earliest software and hardware in the United States.

One of the first applications for this computing capability was with the **new** U.S. **Census** in 1951, which relied on an early version of a computer database called **UNIVAC**, regarded as the world's first commercial computer.

LANCZOS, KRYLOV, HESTENES AND STIEFEL

Cornelius **Lanczos**, a Hungarian, developed several new uses for algorithmic computing throughout the 1950s and 1960s, as well as the mathematical technology that allows us to zoom in and out of digital images and videos.

One of Lanczos's methods, known as **Krylov**, was a collaboration between himself and Magnus **Hestenes** and Eduard **Stiefel** in the 1950s. The Krylov algorithm was named the algorithm of the century because it led to foundational elements behind the scale at which computers can sift through information.

SEAC, UNIVAC, FBI AND FINGERPRINTS

SEAC, or Standards Eastern Automatic Computer, was one of the first computers that could be accessed remotely, created for government use in 1964.

Also around this time, the **FBI** started using the early computing technology to digitize its database of **fingerprints**.

BROOKS ACT, MAGIC FACTS, CHURCHILL EISENHART

In 1964, the **Brooks Act** established automatic data-processing standards, and the federal government launched the first **MAGIC** terminal, one of the earliest computers to use graphics to display information. **Churchill Eisenhart**, a mathematician and chief of the U.S. statistical engineering laboratory, advocated for the federal government to favor "sound mathematical analysis [over] costly experimentation."

FIPS 1, CST, RAILROAD CLUB AT MIT

The first incarnation of the Federal Information Processing Standards (or **FIPS**) was published in 1968, followed by several standards on encryption and data security throughout the 1970s that would underpin the field of cybersecurity into the twenty-first century.

CST probably refers to the Computer Sciences and Technology Lab. One of its first publications, in 1978, is "Effective Use of Computer Technology in Vote-Tallying," which focuses on accuracy and security controls in vote counting done by computer.

The Tech Model **Railroad Club** at the Massachusetts Institute of Technology (**MIT**), which formed in 1946, became a hotbed of early hacker activities in the 1970s and early 1980s, a result of actual model railroad enthusiasts' interest in "signals and power" circuits and switches that make the trains run. This group utilized the term "hacker" in its current form as early as the 1940s.

VOTE COUNTS, JARGON FILE, LINUX KERNEL ONE

Electronic voting has a long history in the United States going back to the 1960s. By the 1980s, several states, wary of traditional punch-card systems, began favoring electronic readers for counting vote cards and punch ballots.

The **jargon file** is a record of hacker lingo first developed at Stanford in the mid-1970s. It records the history and development of casual cybersecurity terms. The first **Linux kernel**, version 0.01, an open-source computer code, was released in 1991 by **Linus** Torvalds.

BILL JOY, LARRY WALL, LINUS, GUIDO VAN ROSSUM

Bill Joy was a cofounder in 1982 of Sun Microsystems, an early computer company. Around the same time, **Larry Wall** was developing Perl, an influential computer language. Linus Torvalds is mentioned above, and **Guido van Rossum** developed the Python programming language, one of the most popular languages today.

CAPTAIN CRUNCH, MA BELL, TWENTY-SIX HUNDRED

John Draper, aka **Captain Crunch**, was an early and influential hacker, part of a loose collective that referred to themselves as Phone Phreaks because they used telephones to hack into various organizations through the phone lines, especially those owned by the Bell Telephone Company, aka **Ma Bell**. The **2600** was a magazine catering to phreaks and other early hackers that detailed how to achieve various malicious activities. Founded in 1984, the title refers to the 2600-hertz tone, which hackers found could be replicated with a toy whistle found inside Cap'n Crunch cereal boxes.

Sources

My observations and conclusions in *Kingdom of Lies* are based exclusively on unclassified, open-source information; my personal observations; and my interviews with individuals who claim knowledge of specific events. None of the information in this book involved access to classified intelligence.

PROLOGUE TO CHAPTER 5

Seleznev, Roman. (2017, April 21). "Roman Seleznev Letter." *New York Times*. www.nytimes.com/interactive/2017/04/21/technology/document-Seleznev-Letter.html.

U.S. Attorney's Office for the Northern District of Georgia. (2017, May 19). "Convicted Russian Cyber Criminal Roman Seleznev Faces Charges in Atlanta." www.justice.gov/usao-ndga/pr/convicted-russian-cyber-criminal-roman-seleznev-faces-charges-atlanta.

CHAPTERS 6 TO 10

Bhattacharjee, Yudhijit. (2011, January 31). "How a Remote Town in Romania Has Become Cybercrime Central." *Wired*. www.wired.com/2011/01/ff-hackerville-romania/.

Carr, Jeffrey. (2011). *Inside Cyber Warfare: Mapping the Cyber Underworld*. Sebastopol, CA: O'Reilly Media.

Healey, Jason. (2013). *A Fierce Domain: Conflicts in Cyberspace 1986 to 2012.* Cyber Conflict Studies Association.

Hinsley, F. H. (1979). *British Intelligence in the Second World War: Its Influence on Strategy and Operations.* London: Stationery Office Books.

Mandiant/FireEye. (2013). "APT1: Exposing One of China's Cyber Espionage Units." www.fireeye.com/content/dam/fireeye-www/services/pdfs/mandiant-apt1-report.pdf.

Usdin, Steven T. (2005). *Engineering Communism: How Two Americans Spied for Stalin and Founded the Soviet Silicon Valley.* Binghamton, NY: Vale-Ballou Press.

CHAPTERS 11 TO 16

Department of Justice. (2017, November 27). "U.S. Charges Three Chinese Hackers Who Work at Internet Security Firm for Hacking Three Corporations for Commercial Advantage." www.justice.gov/opa/pr/us-charges-three-chinese-hackers-who-work-internet-security-firm-hacking-three-corporations.

Department of Justice. (2014, May 19). "U.S. Charges Five Chinese Military Hackers for Cyber Espionage Against U.S. Corporations and a Labor Organization for Commercial Advantage: First Time Criminal Charges Are Filed Against Known State Actors for Hacking." www.justice.gov/opa/pr/us-charges-five-chinese-military-hackers-cyber-espionage-against-us-corporations-and-labor.

Trustwave. (2017). "Post-Soviet Bank Heists: A Hybrid Cybercrime Study." www2.trustwave.com/Post-Soviet-Bank-Heists-Report.html.

Wang, Helen. (2004). *Money on the Silk Road: The Evidence from Eastern Central Asia to c. AD 800.* London: British Museum Press.

Whitfield, Susan. (2018). *Silk, Slaves and Stupas: Material Culture of the Silk Road.* Oakland: University of California Press.

CHAPTERS 17 TO EPILOGUE

Department of Justice. (2018, July 13). "Grand Jury Indicts 12 Russian Intelligence Officers for Hacking Offenses Related to the 2016 Election." https://www.justice.gov/opa/pr/grand-jury-indicts-12-russian-intelligence-officers-hacking-offenses-related-2016-election.

Department of Justice. (2015, October 15). "ISIL-Linked Hacker Arrested in Malaysia on U.S. Charges (with complaint)." www.justice.gov/opa/pr/isil-linked-hacker-arrested-malaysia-us-charges.

Hadnagy, Christopher. (2018). *Social Engineering: The Science of Human Hacking*. Indianapolis: Wiley.

Næringslivets Sikkerhetsråd. (2016, September). "Norwegian Computer Crime and Data Breach Survey 2016. Mørketallundersøkelsen 2016." www.nsr-org.no/getfile.php/Bilder/M%C3%B8rketallsunders%C3%B8kelsen/morketallsundersokelsen_2016_eng.pdf.

National Institute for Standards in Technology. (Created October 12, 2010; updated August 27, 2018). "ITL History Timeline 1950–2018." www.nist.gov/itl/about-itl/itl-history-timeline.

U.S. Attorney's Office for the Southern District of New York. (2015, November 10). "Attorney General and Manhattan U.S. Attorney Announce Charges Stemming from Massive Network Intrusions at U.S. Financial Institutions, U.S. Brokerage Firms, a Major News Publication, and Other Companies." www.justice.gov/usao-sdny/pr/attorney-general-and-manhattan-us-attorney-announce-charges-stemming-massive-network.

Author's Note

Thank you for taking the time to read this book.

I didn't set out to write a book, certainly not after I joined the cybersecurity field. I wanted to leave my brief, youthful background as a journalist behind and do something real. And I did.

As I wrote in the beginning, that's when I noticed the holes in the narrative we have grown to accept about security and insecurity of technology, and the real people who were working in or even leading various factions within it.

WHAT JUST HAPPENED?

After going to work for *The Wall Street Journal*, I was mostly prohibited from using anonymous sources, which is a good thing and strengthens news coverage. But it also meant that the majority of people I talked to would never see their names—or pseudonyms—in print.

This book gave me the flexibility to tell controversial stories, or see events through the eyes of people who lived them. I acknowledge that these people might not always have told the truth. My father, a Navy vet, once said that sailors had a tendency to tell tall tales, and here we are looking through the lens of sailors on a rough, digital sea.

You may also note that I've fictionalized some locations—such as Arnica Valka, Romania, which does not exist—but kept other real locations. In some cases, creating fictional locations or companies was the only way to adequately convey the story while ensuring that I was protecting the identity of sources and other innocent parties.

WHY DOES IT MATTER?

I'm completing this book after yet another contentious election—the US 2018 midterms. There will be more. Some predicted this election would be "the World Cup of cyber influence." Another lie, of course. Our elections boards did a fine job of mucking up local elections without needing any interference from Russian elites. Just another in a long line of dire predictions that we have somehow turned a corner into a heretofore unimagined apocalypse.

The idea we are somehow in a strange and very different time is dangerous for three reasons. One, it negates history and historians unfairly, as if all knowledge we've acquired up until this moment is meaningless in the face of this new threat. Two, it gives governments, corporations, and institutions an out that they don't deserve—specifically, the excuse that things have become so incomprehensible and troubling that they can't possibly be expected to fight against them. And three, it makes people feel helpless, as if they can have no part in understanding security or threats, working on it or having opinions on it, because it's all so new and frightening that trying to grasp it won't matter.

If I could support any outcome of reading this book, it is that people feel more empowered to make decisions in their lives that support their own best idea of personal privacy. And that they feel empowered to hold governments, media, and institutions accountable for doing their jobs and providing them with timely, accurate, and actionable information.

Above all, I hope people can start to see that what is happening is more like decades of erosion and less like having the ground disappear from underneath our feet. And that there are ways to stop erosion.

Acknowledgments

First and foremost, I'd like to thank Elisabeth Dyssegaard from St. Martin's Press and Peter McGuigan from Foundry Literary Media—and all of their staff—for taking a chance on this first-time author. To the people who made endorsements for this book, it's meant so much to me—thank you.

For their support in trying to turn me into a proper journalist: Matt Rossoff, Jeff McCracken, Mike Calia, Mary Duffy, Elisabeth Cordova, Lauren Hirsch, and Steve Kovach from CNBC; Ben DiPietro, Nick Elliott, Rob Sloan, Will Wilkinson, and Kim Nash from *The Wall Street Journal*; and Ken Clark, Allan Ripp, John Garger, and Paul Comstock.

I'd like to thank several people who were incredibly supportive during my time working on this book, earlier in my career, and through some trying experiences—without whom it wouldn't have been possible: Judith Pinto, Jennifer Flores, Jamal Raghei, and Britt-Louise Gilder; Seth Kaufman, Elena Tisnovsky, Victoria and Justin Meyer, Amy Edelstein, Frederic Lemieux, Susanne Gutermuth, Ida Piasevoli, Ang Johnson, Steven Greene, Pete Cavicchia, Anish Bhimani, Michael Spadea, Marc Loewenthal, Mike Joseph, and Earl Crane.

There are many people who served as anonymous sources for this book who I can't name here, but I would like to acknowledge: thank you for taking a risk and telling me your stories.

To Mrs. Belcastro, Miss Kristy, and all the staff and teachers at PS 002 in Queens and New Milestone Preschool for their incredible work with my kids.

To the staff at Porto Bello Restaurant in Astoria, Queens, for their patience and excellent Wi-Fi.

Thanks to all my teachers who made my life better, especially Tim Henige, Paul McClintock, Tim Rice, and Cindy Polles.

And, of course, Mom and Dad and sister Ann for their enduring and life-long support.

Index